THE
PRIVATE JOURNAL
OF
F. S. LARPENT,
JUDGE-ADVOCATE GENERAL OF THE BRITISH FORCES
IN THE PENINSULA
ATTACHED TO THE HEAD-QUARTERS OF
LORD WELLINGTON DURING THE PENINSULAR WAR,
FROM 1812 TO ITS CLOSE

VOLUME II

Elibron Classics
www.elibron.com

Elibron Classics series.

© 2006 Adamant Media Corporation.

ISBN 1-4021-8871-4 (paperback)
ISBN 1-4212-9606-3 (hardcover)

This Elibron Classics Replica Edition is an unabridged facsimile
of the edition published in 1853 by Richard Bentley, London.

PRIVATE JOURNAL.

THE

PRIVATE JOURNAL

OF

F. S. LARPENT, ESQ.,

JUDGE ADVOCATE GENERAL OF THE BRITISH FORCES

IN THE PENINSULA.

ATTACHED TO THE HEAD-QUARTERS OF

LORD WELLINGTON DURING THE PENINSULAR WAR,

FROM 1812 TO ITS CLOSE.

EDITED

BY SIR GEORGE LARPENT, BART.

IN THREE VOLUMES.
VOL. II.

LONDON:

RICHARD BENTLEY, NEW BURLINGTON STREET,

Publisher in Ordinary to Her Majesty.

MDCCCLIII.

CONTENTS OF VOLUME II.

PAGE

CHAPTER I.

Movements of the army—Wellington on the Portuguese—His personal habits—St. Sebastian—The
siege—Miseries of war—Wounded officers—The
Prince of Orange—Vestiges of the retreat—English
papers—False accounts of the campaign—Incidents
of the war 1

CHAPTER II.

Rejoicings for the victory—Sufferings of Cole's division—Complaints of the French—Statements of a
French prisoner—Decay of Spain—Characteristics
of Wellington—His opinion of Bonaparte—Prospects of a renewal of the attack—Exchange of
prisoners — Wellington's Spanish estate — His
opinion of Picton—Disposition of the army . . 38

PAGE
CHAPTER III.

Reported renewal of operations against St. Sebastian—
Effects of the war on Spain and Portugal—Wellington's account of recent proceedings—Courts-martial—Prisoners shot—Discussions on war between
Wellington and a French deserter—The siege resumed—Work of the heavy batteries—Trial of
General O'Halloran—Volunteers for the storming
parties   65

CHAPTER IV.

The Author taken prisoner—Kind treatment by the
French General—Life of a prisoner—Release—De-
tails of the Author's captivity—Curious scene at
General Pakenham's—A Basque squire .   .   . 83

CHAPTER V.

Picturesque quarters—Spanish reverses—A strange
adventure—Spanish jealousy—Distribution of the
army—A pleasant companion—News from the
North—Morale of the French army—The artillery 121

CHAPTER VI.

Fall of Pamplona—Deterioration of the army—Duke
of York's orders—Orders of merit—Church service
—Capture of French redoubts—March of the army
—Incidents of foreign service—Frequency of desertion—Wellington and the lawyers 143

PAGE
CHAPTER VII.

News from France—Lord Fitzroy Somerset—Departure of the Prince of Orange—Exchange of prisoners —Proximity of the two armies—Wellington's cooks — Warlike movements — French attack — The Guards—Deserters—More fighting   .   .   . 174

CHAPTER VIII.

French attack—Plan of desertion—Excesses of the French — A Basque witness—Sir John Hope — Movements of the army—Sale of effects—Wellington's simplicity of character—A French emigré— Return of Soult to Bayonne 196

CHAPTER IX.

Reports from France—More desertion—Anecdote of General Stewart—Wellington and his casualty returns—The courtesies of war—Scarcity of transports—Wellington and the trial-papers—Sir G. Collier   219

CHAPTER X.

Rumours of war—The rival dinner tables—" Slender Billy "—Bonaparte's trickery—Spanish violence— Wellington with the hounds—French and English aspects—The outsides of the nations   .   .   . 239

PAGE

CHAPTER XI.

State of feeling in France — Rocket-practice — The Prince Regent's hobby—The Mayor's ball—The flag-of-truce 253

CHAPTER XII.

Army supplies — Offending villages — Symptoms of work — Arrival of the Duke d'Angoulême — The bridge across the Adour—Wellington and his chief engineer—His activity 276

PRIVATE JOURNAL,

&c. &c.

***

CHAPTER I.

MOVEMENTS OF THE ARMY—WELLINGTON ON THE PORTU-
GUESE — HIS PERSONAL HABITS — ST. SEBASTIAN — THE
SIEGE — MISERIES OF WAR — WOUNDED OFFICERS — THE
PRINCE OF ORANGE—VESTIGES OF THE RETREAT—ENGLISH
PAPERS—FALSE ACCOUNTS OF THE CAMPAIGN—INCIDENTS
OF THE WAR.

Head-Quarters, Lezaca,
July 21, 1813.

MY DEAR M——,

HERE we are still, deluged with rain almost
incessantly, accompanied at times with violent storms
of wind, hail, and thunder. This is terrible for the
troops in camp, and for every one more or less, and
indeed for everything except the Indian corn, which
thrives here most luxuriantly in consequence of
this perpetual wet. I took my ride (the 19th) up

to the hill above the seventh division as I intended;
it was a league and a half, and the latter part very
steep. The French were in sight all along the
hills, the other side of Bera, all around one ridge,
but quite quiet. When at the summit I saw the
sea-coast around Bayonne (though not the town
itself), and the low country in France, for I suppose
thirty miles inland, with the enclosed fields, villages, &c.: it was a very fine prospect; I was only
sorry to see that the French had apparently so
much more productive a country immediately
in their rear than we had. They must now however
be supplied at the **expense** of old France. We are
but ill off here for **everything** just now, until our
supplies come regularly to this coast.

Passages is to be the depôt and landing-place,
I hear, for our infantry, and Bilbao for cavalry.
Major-general Lord Aylmer is to-day setting off
to take a command at Passages; he expects nearly
four thousand men there very soon. We still hear
the battering guns of St. Sebastian continually roaring at a distance; I fear we may lose many men in
this siege. Good luck however may do something
for us, and the French seem everywhere dispirited;
sickness, at present, if this **weather** lasts, will be
our most destructive foe.

Suchet, I hear, has left a garrison at Murviedro,

when he crossed the Ebro. They seem to have intended to give us some tough work until they were ready to return; I hope here, at least, that will not be so easy. Both sides are now strongly posted, and the attacker must, I think, have the worst of it. Soult is said to have refused to take the command of the army here, unless the pay of the troops was more regular. Lord Wellington talking of this paid the highest compliment to Bonaparte, by saying, that if he came himself, he should, as he always did, reckon his presence as a reinforcement of forty thousand men, for that it would give a turn to everything.

Lord Wellington, talking of the Portuguese, said, it was extraordinary just now, to observe their conduct—that no troops could behave better, that they never had now a notion of turning, and that nothing could be like their forwardness now, and willing, ready, tempers. I am sorry to say that some of our foreign corps do not go on as well. Of the Brunswick corps, ten went off from picket two nights since to the French, and fourteen from the camp, and others have gone off also, and some have been surprised, so that I believe they are ordered to be sent more to the rear and cannot be trusted; I do not wonder at it, as government have taken men from the French prisons, who

were only taken last year, and who, I have no
doubt, only enlisted on purpose to desert the first
opportunity.

Lezaca, July 22nd.—To-day Lord Wellington
celebrates Salamanca by a great dinner. His victories and successes will soon ruin him, in wine
and eating, and if he goes on as he has, he had
better keep open house at once every day, and his
calendar of feasts will be as full as the Romish one,
with red letter days. This morning the guns have
been thundering salvoes. I think the breach must
be ready soon. I only hope we shall not lose many
of our fine fellows. Pamplona is invested more
closely, that is all that is attempted; two sallies
have been repulsed ; there are about fifteen thousand Spaniards there. I was sorry to hear, that
very lately bread was in the town the same price
as when we were first there, and that a low Spanish
price ; this does not look much like starving the
garrison out. For a regular siege we have no means,
and the place is formidable from the very circum-
stance that makes it look otherwise—the citadel is
all flat, there is nothing to fire at, and no ground
to approach it by. The scenery all about this lower
Pyrenees and coast, is like the north coast of Devonshire and Somersetshire, a little enlarged as you
get inland, and so increasing in size, but the same

character remaining for a considerable extent, only the valleys becoming deeper, and the hills higher. There is nothing however as striking here as the passage of the Ebro and the valley near where we crossed it.

Major D—— has still got his prize here taken on the field of battle, namely, a Spanish girl, a pony, the wardrobe, monkey, &c., the property of one of king Joseph's aides-de-camp. I am still kept at work. We yesterday tried two men for plundering Lord Aylmer's tent in the night whilst he slept, and I have a man to try for a rape at Urdug. He says he thought it was France, and that there it was all regular.

Out of 500,000*l.* sterling supposed to be plundered at Vittoria, only about 30,000*l.* has found its way to the treasury, or military chest. Lord Wellington seems to think the best of Mina, Longa, and the Empecinado ; amongst the Spaniards there is much to be done yet, to make them like our vagabonds or the Portuguese, as to fighting ; for plundering and the " *savoir vivre* " here without money or rations, they beat us both already ; we cannot improve them.

Castanos, the other day at dinner, asked Lord Wellington how Madame Gazan had been treated, as she was accustomed to have a considerable number of lovers ? Lord Wellington looked rather drolly at me, and said, she had been treated, he believed, very properly and respectfully. Castanos said, " *Elle en serait bien fâché.*"

Last week some of the light division had rations of wheat in the grain instead of bread. One fellow, who was sulky, said, he supposed he should have " long forage" next, that is, straw. Another more good humouredly said, he was as strong as a horse now since yesterday. How so ? " Why, they have given me a good feed of corn you see, so how could it be otherwise." We had one very ingenious device by two of our fellows last week ; they were employed to take care of two thousand dollars prize, for the benefit of the regiment, and to carry it on a mule or ass given to them for that purpose. General Cole passed this donkey on a bridge, and being irritated from the obstruction caused by the baggage, &c., swore he would upset the whole over the bridge if they were not off, &c. When he had passed, one said, " That will just do, let's divide the money, and say the General upset it in the river." This was done and the report made ; something, however, was overheard, and this led to an inquiry, and one admitted that this was the case, and that a serjeant shared and proposed the plan. I said I could only get them flogged for this. Lord Wellington therefore said they might as well be tried in their regiment, as three hundred lashes was as good as a thousand, and publishing these things only put similar ideas into other people's heads.

Lezaca, Head-Quarters, July 23rd.—Lord Wellington and all his party went off at eight this morning for St. Sebastian to see how things are going on. He intends returning to dinner, a late one I think it will be, though they all have fresh horses on the road. It is feared his hints have not been attended to, I believe, and that the breach has been made too soon before all other things were ready, so that the place of danger is discovered to the enemy in time, perhaps, to enable the French, who are ever quick and ready on these occasions, to let in some sea, and make a wet ditch behind, or to throw up new works, &c. The breach may thus, as at Badajoz, become the worst place of the whole to attack. I hope this is only a false alarm; but things, I think, do not go on well, unless Lord Wellington or General Murray are on the spot Lord Wellington is not as easily roused from his bed as he used to be. This is the only change in him; and it is said he has been in part encouraged to this by having such confidence in General Murray. I understand he was always naturally fond of his pillow. He had rather ride like an

express for ten or fifteen leagues, than be early
and take time to his work. Upon the whole this
may fatigue him less, as being a less time on horseback.

Head-Quarters, Lezaca, July 25th, 1813.—We
have now been some time stationary in these
mountains, and I am at work again, and have little
time, and less to write about. We have been here
in hourly expectation of the nervous news of the
storming of St. Sebastian. It was first to have
taken place the day before yesterday; but things
were not quite ready; then at five yesterday morning; but either from our shells firing a house near
the breach, and the French encouraging the flames
to spread, or from their originally setting fire to
that part of the town, there was such a considerable fire all around the breach, that it was thought
too hot for storming. It was then, by Lord Wellington's order, I believe, fixed for this morning,
and he has been as usual very anxious about the
event.

I saw he was very fidgetty yesterday, when I
went to him about two poor fellows who are to be
hung for robbing Lord Aylmer's tent; and to-day
he came out to the church-yard, where we were
listening, about eight o'clock, to judge from the
noise of the guns whether our batteries had ceased

and what the firing was. He has been once over himself, but seemed to wish to leave it to Graham, and not to interfere immediately. At eleven this morning, however, came over Colonel Burgh, with an account of our attempt having failed; that our party (consisting of English, too, and I believe of the 9th and 38th) went up to the breach, then turned, and ran away. This will terribly discourage our fellows who have to go next, and encourage the enemy. Lord Wellington has ordered his horse, and is going over immediately, I hear.

Nothing can be done, however, before the evening or to-morrow morning, as the attack must take place within two hours before or after low water, in order to pass the sands for the breach. I am told the latter is wide and easy, and we cannot tell what came to our fellows on this occasion. The object, St. Sebastian, is a most important one for the army; first, if we are to keep our ground here, as an *appui* to the left flank, and secondly as a safe place for stores, sick, wounded, &c., where, in case of retreat, they may be all left to be got off at leisure by sea, and also as a refuge for Guerillas, &c. We begin to get a few things brought to us in these wild inhospitable regions, but still from Lisbon by land, with the six weeks' carriage on a mule to pay for. If some one would speculate to Passages direct it would fully answer, as Irish butter is 4s. 6d. a pound ; sugar, 4s. ; ham, 3s. ; tea, 20s., the same as that sold at Lisbon for 8s. ; and so on.

To-day I am going about three miles up the Bidassoa river to a passada, in which the artillery of Colonel Rosse's troops are quartered, to dine with them. Part of the way to their present quarters from St. Estevan they had to cut their road with spades and pickaxes for the guns ; but there they now are safe.

I am sorry to say several of our men (English) desert as well as the foreigners. I have just heard that the cause of their failure at St. Sebastian this morning was partly the same as that of Badajoz formerly—a deep ditch behind the breach, and nothing to fill it up with, if that were possible ; but it is said to have been very deep. Our fellows looked, came back, got for shelter under the wall, and were then ordered back, and they ran a little. This is a much better account of the business. The attack was also too soon, so that the tide prevented one attack from being attempted, and it is feared our artillery even fired from that cause on the attackers. The French certainly understand sieges better, I think, than we do.

Head-Quarters, Berrio Planca, in front of

Pamplona, half a league, July 31st, 1813.—To my great surprise, here I am again, and I must now tell you how and why.

Head-Quarters, again at Lezaca, near Bera, in the Mountains, August 3rd, 1813.—I had just taken up this paper, and headed it as above, to begin my history, when a turn of good fortune arising from the courage of our army, and from the superior manœuvres of our General, have in eight days brought head-quarters back to our old place, from whence the first sheet of this letter was dated. I have been too much occupied in this interval almost to sit down, much more to write; but I will try and detail the important events I have witnessed in them in the best order my recollection will permit.

On the 25th July I went over, as I intended to dine with the artillery. About seven I mounted to return home, Colonel Ross, Captains Jenkinson and Belson riding with me. We met a messenger. With my usual curiosity I asked him to whom he was going? He said to Colonel Ross. The Colonel was called back. He found it was an order to march that night, and rather to the rear. There had been a distant firing all day, on the right wing near Maya. Lord Wellington was over at St. Sebastian. Belson was sent to General Alten

with orders by Colonel Ross. Jenkinson galloped
back to order the troops to get ready. Colonel
Ross begged me to tell General Murray he would
try and reach Sambillo that night, gave a receipt
for the letter, and was off. When I returned I
found Lord Wellington still absent, and reports
flying about, but no orders. I soon found, however, that things were not right, and ordered everything to be ready for the march next morning.
Lord Wellington returned to dinner at eight, and
found the following account of matters on our right
just arrived to greet him on his return from the
failure of St. Sebastian.

The French had collected a force both at the
Roncesvalles pass against General Cole, and at the
Maya pass against General Hill. In the morning
of the 25th they pushed a strong reconnoissance
against General Stewart, commanding Hill's advance brigade near Maya, made a show, but gave
way again ; this report we had heard, and thought
all was over. About three, however, the French
advanced against Cole and Hill. About twenty-
two thousand against Cole's force, about sixteen
thousand against General Stewart's brigade ; the
latter had his force scattered on the hills round
the pass. The French came up in one close body,
and gradually ascended the hill. Our people fired

on them the whole time, and the destruction was very considerable. They still, however, gained ground. They were twice charged by a single regiment of ours, and the head of the column gave a little, but the press of numbers urged them on, and as our force was only about three thousand men, and that acting only by small bodies of regiments or companies, the French drove all before them after a most gallant but fatal resistance, before a sufficient reinforcement could be brought up. Four Portuguese guns were abandoned. Our loss in killed and wounded you will see in the "*Gazette.*" It is said to be twelve hundred British, almost all in three or four regiments—principally the 50th, 92nd, 74th, and 28th. In the 92nd, I am told, there was no officer except the Quarter-Master in a state to march off the men at parade· Colonel Belson (28th) had only four officers left besides himself on duty, as he had been thinned at Vittoria. To add to this disaster, General Cole thought he was not justified in opposing the superior force against him, and gave way in the Roncesvalles pass. This left an opening to get in the rear of General Hill in the valley of Bastan at Elisondo. Of course, therefore, he was obliged to fall back also, and the result was that Lord Wellington on his return found his right wing forced, and his position completely turned. Retreat, and that a rapid one, became necessary, to take a new position, and to fall back on the divisions near Pamplona.

After I was in bed on the night of the 25th the order came to march, as I expected. Lord Wellington was off early straight across to the second division. The light divisions fell back from our front; the seventh also toward St. Estevan towards the second; the artillery proceeded to St. Estevan by Sumbillo. Head-quarters were sent over the mountains by Yanga and Aranor to a little village called Eligarraga, just as you descend into the valley of St. Estevan, there to wait full orders.

We had a wild and tedious road of four leagues up and down the mountains like Blue Beard's procession, in which we should now all be adepts. There was a road round the bottom through Sumbillo, but I conclude that was not thought safe, and that it might interfere with the artillery, as it was narrow the whole way, and nothing could pass.

About two o'clock on the 26th we reached Eligarraga, and there found Major Canning sitting by the way side to order every thing on three long leagues further through Estevan, and then after keeping the road along the valley about a league beyond towards the pass into the Bastan Valley, near Trinita and Elisondo, we were to turn at Oronoz through a pass on the right, which brought us into the rear of the valley of Bastan, and into the rear of General Hill's division to a place called Almendoz, on the road to Pamplona from Elisondo, General Hill having his head-quarters half a league in our present rear as we retreated, at our old head-quarters, Berrueta. In the mean time the seventh and light divisions got down into the valley of St. Estevan that night.

At Almendoz we found the effects of our battle at Maya. The wounded had just reached that place, and there those who had not been dressed, had their wounds examined, and all were urged on to the rear over a mountain-pass to Lanz as fast as possible. The village of Almendoz was very small; the wounded lying about in all directions, till cars and mules could help them on. It was near seven o'clock, and we had nothing to eat since seven in the morning, quarters very bad of course, and the inhabitants all in the greatest distress, beginning to pack up, to desert their houses, as the people in the valley of Bastan, at Elisondo, &c., had done already, the French having got possession. A retreat is a most distressing scene even at the best, and when conducted with perfect order as this was.

About nine o'clock that night orders came to
march at daylight for Ulague, a place about half-
way between Lanz and Ostig.   After a five o'clock
breakfast, which I now always get of tea, away we
went for our mountains again.   The road was
choked with baggage, and artillery, and fugitives,
amongst others, fourteen or fifteen nuns in their
dresses, who were reduced by fatigue to beg some
rum of us as we passed, which unfortunately we
had not with us.   We got on by scrambling along
the paths near the road, and arrived about twelve.
On the 27th we arrived at Lanz.   We there found
General Murray and several officers, all looking
very serious and gloomy, and orders given for
everything to be turned off that road to the right,
and not to go to Ulague, as Cole had been pressed.
The firing was very sharp, and the French were
urging on to that road, besides which, by taking to
the right we got towards the *camino real*, from
Pamplona to Tolosa, and could have made for
General Graham's if necessary.   We were turned
through Arayes (where I had been on the advance,
and by the road where I had lost myself before in
the night), on through a rich valley and several
villages to Lissago, or Ligasso.

Here (the 27th), we were placed very snug, only
about two leagues and a-half from the Tolosa road,

about three from Pamplona, and in the midst of the
divisions. General Cole, with the fourth division,
had fallen back on Pamplona to some hills near
Villa Alba, or Vilalba : there he joined the third
division, General Picton's, and some Spaniards.
General Hill fell back to Lanz. From Berrueta,
the seventh division got a short way over the
mountains, from St. Estevan to near Ligasso, our
head-quarters, and thus got near the sixth. The
light division fell back more towards Goigueta,
or Ernani, to communicate with Graham and
protect the Tolosa road, and thus we stood all
night.

The scene at Ligasso was dreadful! All the
wounded from Lanz were just arrived there, in
cars, on mules, crawling on crutches, and hobbling
along ; all those with the wounds in their hands
and arms, &c., walking. Finding they had orders
to stop there, all our quarters, except Lord Wellington's, and about four more houses, were given
up, and we all dispersed to the villages round.
You may conceive the scene, both on the road and
in the village. I thought I had lost one of my
horse's shoes on the road, and desired my servant
to ascertain the point. A soldier walking along,
apparently one of the best, said, I had not; that
he was still, as a farrier, able to see that, though he

thought he should be some months before he should
put another shoe on, as he had been shot through
the back. I went with Colonel and Mrs. Scovell
to a little village, half-way up the hill towards
Pamplona; and Colonel Scovell and I climbed up
to the top of the hill to listen and look about until
nearly six o'clock, when we expected our baggage.
The curé of the village and three peasants went up
with us. We could see over beyond Pamplona,
and beyond the firing, but could not quite see the
place itself for the smoke. By five o'clock, however, we all agreed that it slackened, and receded
a little; we therefore descended, got a beef-steak,
and waited ready for orders.

About six that evening the wounded were ordered to move on towards Inerzun, on the Vittoria
and Tolosa roads; but we remained quiet. About
seven, a furious thunder-storm came on, and caught
all our poor wounded men on their march: they
could not get on to Inerzun, but got to Berrio
Planca, near Pamplona. Two officers, one sick
and one wounded in a house half a mile from us,
heard of this order, left their beds, packed up, and
were proceeding. They came to us to inquire.
We said head-quarters were not to move. They
went back to bed, keeping a guide in the house all
night, to start in case of alarm. At nine came an

order to march to Orcayen, near Pamplona, the next morning. Thus passed the 27th.

At five o'clock on the 28th I began to load to proceed to Orcayen, when Mr. Hook, who takes quarters, came back and left word that we were to go to Inerzun instead ; but the serjeant, by mistake, told us he would call again when he had made more inquiry. In consequence of this Mrs. Scovell and I staid until past ten before we marched. Then, finding every one gone, and the baggage of General Hill's division arrived at Ligasso, we started over the mountain. For the first league, we got quite right ; but afterwards, in a wood, got too much to the right, and entered a wrong valley : as it was all safe, however, to blunder on that side, and the country was pretty, we went on that road, and by this means got through to Oscoz, and came into the high Pamplona road to Tolosa, about three-quarters of a league from Inerzun towards Tolosa, instead of half a league on the Pamplona side of Inerzun, which would have been the nearest ; it was not a league round, and very picturesque. We were, therefore, not sorry for the mistake. At Inerzun, however, came a difficulty ; it was quite crowded with wounded. Of headquarters we could hear nothing, nor of our baggage.

I left my servant to bring on the baggage if it

came, and we proceeded forwards towards Pamplona, near where we heard head-quarters were—somewhere at least that way. At Berrio Planca, a place on the *camino real*, we found all our baggage and the nominal head-quarters. Every one, however, was absent, and the place full of wounded, the effects of the preceding day. I got a room in the Prince of Orange's quarters, as he had sent for his bed away that night; but Henry had all my keys. About seven, however, I got a beefsteak at a friend's; at eight found Henry and went to bed.

The next morning, the 29th, I heard we had the most severe work on the 28th; that the French attacked six or seven times our position on a hill, which I believe our troops had only occupied a few hours before the French came up near Oraquin, or Orquin. These attacks were quite desperate; and I understand that such a fire was scarcely ever known for a short time, as four French corps all bore upon one point, and General Pakenham told me he scarcely dared show any of his men. These attacks were, however, all unsuccessful, and we kept our ground. The French were generally driven down with the bayonet, having been suffered to come close, and then received with a volley, a cheer, and a charge. I hear some of our officers were once very much alarmed. The French remained close and steady, and our regiment (I believe the 40th) went at them rather loose and straggling. However, at the cheer at the last moment the French broke and ran. The Portuguese behaved in general most inimitably, the 4th, 10th, and 12th regiments in particular. The 10th did, indeed, once give way, but rallied ; and the 4th charged twice, I think, on the 27th June, in high English style.

Our loss was very severe ; that of the French, of course, much more so ; but as their cavalry carry off the wounded to the rear, and they have an hospital corps also for that purpose, no one knows their losses ; their prisoners and deserters say nearly five thousand. Lord Wellington's staff were never so roughly handled. The Prince of Orange, who was sent to thank one regiment by Lord Wellington, was very much exposed in executing this order. His horse was shot under him, and he was grazed in the sash. It was near this place that General's Cole's aide-de-camp had been killed, and also Brigade-Major A——, one of my Deputy Judge-Advocates. He was trying to rally a Spanish battalion, which was quite broken. The Adjutant-general Pakenham had his coat sleeve torn considerably by a ball. Colonel Waters, A.A.G.C., was shot in the head, through the hat,

on the temple, but somehow was little hurt. It is
thought the ball glanced under the hat, against
the head, and passed out through the hat. He
was out again the next day. Lord Wellington was
near at the time, and told him his head must be
like a rock.

Lord Wellington said, I hear, he had never seen
the French behave better. He staid and dined at
Picton's on the 28th, and few returned to head-quarters. All the 29th was quiet; both sides employed
burying the dead and getting off the wounded.
On the 29th also the staff and light canteens alone
remained at Villalba with General Cole; and I
was left with scarcely anything except wounded
men and baggage. All the stores were ordered to
be unloaded, and all spare mules of the head-
quarters and of the 2nd and 7th divisions likewise.
Two troops of Portuguese cavalry were employed
from daylight to dark, in addition to cars and
hospital waggons, in carrying off the wounded to
Inerzun, to be out of the way in case of attack,
and on the road to the great hospital at Vittoria.

I made myself of some use in assisting the
arrangement, and as there were not hands to move
the men from their mules, to get their rations, &c.,
and then remount them to proceed, I went and
asked an artillery officer close by, to lend some of

his men to assist, which he did directly, and everything went on as quick again. I was sure they
would not stand upon form on such an occasion,
and the men were idle, waiting for orders; they
said they were only sorry it was not known sooner,
and they would have given men all day. The
scene was a busy one. I suppose nearly twelve
hundred went through in this way; they were
rationed for two days to get on to Echani, mounted
and sent off, their ammunition having in the
meantime been taken from them to be better
used, as that was getting scarce more than once
Some had two, some one ball still in them.
Besides this, at home I had Colonel Campbell of
the Portuguese service, wounded and lying in my
ante-room all day. He was shot through the shin-
bone, a painful wound; he could not get into my
room, which of course I offered, but preferred the
cool passage. I was at breakfast when he arrived.
I gave him tea, and some newspapers to try and
read himself to sleep. A friend was with him,
a Campbell, who shared my bouillie; he ate as
good a dinner as I did, but objected to a second
bottle, upon which I discovered he also was
wounded in the side, and feared that the end of his
rib was broken.

The next morning, the 30th, we were all in sus-

pense, as Lord Wellington had determined on a
general attack. The firing began at daylight. At
nine o'clock I determined to go and see what was
going on, and mounting my black, proceeded up
for the hills, where the 6th and 7th divisions were,
which were on the opposite side of the valley from
our grand position, where we had been attacked
the day before. I met many wounded, crawling
back all the way, and on the top found only the
pickets left in the camp of the morning, and that
the seventh division had just driven the French
from the adjoining hill, and were after them up the
valley on the other side. I went on to the point of
the hill and saw the battle still raging strong, just
opposite on the hills below, on the other side of the
valley opposite our position. The French still
steady and firing very briskly all round the side of
one hill and in the village below us, and our people creeping on by degrees under ridges towards
the village and the hill, and also advancing round
the back of the hill; we had two mortars and a
gun also upon our position-hill constantly at work,
playing upon the French line, and we saw the
shells continually fall and burst close to the French
line, whilst the wounded were carried off to the
rear.

This went on some time, above an hour after I

came up, and we had men in reserve all around. I
then saw our fellows in the village, and immediately under the French, and appearing at top
also. The French gave way, but went on firing all
over the hill. In half-an-hour, I heard the loud
huzzas of our soldiers, and saw no French left
except on the next hills, where they seemed very
numerous and strong, but in confusion. The first
huzzas were I believe for a body of about eighteen
hundred prisoners, who were caught, being headed
every way. There was soon a shout on our side
close by our positions, and I saw it was Marshal
Beresford and Lord Wellington proceeding down
to the village to water their horses and proceed on.
I should have wished to have pushed on also, but
I knew head-quarters would move, and had told
my people I should return, and not to stir until I
came back. I therefore went my two leagues back
to Berrio Planca, found as I expected all loaded and
on the move to go towards Orquin ; got a mouth-
ful of mouldy bread in the market and went back
again close to our position at Orquin. There we got
orders to halt loaded, until orders came to proceed
to Ostiz. We took off our bridles, turned the horses
into a field of Indian corn, where the French camp
had been four hours before, and where their dead
of the 28th had been buried. We waited thus

hearing a distant firing until near dark. The reason of this halt, as I learned from General O'Donnell, who passed, was that D'Erlon had attacked
General Hill in the morning, and that he had been
rather too much in advance, and was in some degree
obliged to give way ; that he had taken a new
position, and expected the second attack without
alarm, as he was to be supported.

About four or five thousand Spaniards moved by
us whilst we halted and went up that way. I
conclude that was part of the support alluded to.
General Hill was attacked again, and I understand
beat the Count D'Erlon (Drouet) back with great
loss. When this had put all matters straight again,
on that side, at least, we were to proceed. At last
came orders to advance to Lanz, and we moved
again. We first, however, drew up on one side to
allow eighteen hundred prisoners to march to the
rear,—a very pleasant sight. I spoke to several,
and found all of the 17th regiment, who were
numerous, to be Italians, principally Genoese.
They said they hated the French, but were forced
to fight in Spain against their inclinations. All the
prisoners seemed quite tired of Spain, and were as
anxious as most of our people never to see it again.
They said Soult was more in the rear, and did not
intend to fight that day, which was true, I believe,

as he waited for General D'Erlon to get up from St. Estevan towards Lanz. General Monceau, I believe, commanded.

We were again a second time stopped under some trees, as Lord Wellington had ordered the French to be moved from their position beyond Ostiz, and driven to near Lanz; the baggage was halted till the result was known. In the villages and on the road, which was strewed with pouches, empty knapsacks, and broken muskets, we passed several bodies all stripped, and in some places could scarcely avoid treading on them, by the horse stepping over a leg or an arm. In one place on the road was a half-buried Frenchman, which the horse had again laid bare. The doctors determined to halt, and encamp under some trees; and if my baggage had been near me to stop it, I believe I should have bivouacked with them, as I had no tent. As it was, I proceeded, got a wretched quarter at Ostiz with Colonel Waters and seven country fellows, just come from the mountains, at about nine o'clock, got a beef-steak at eleven, and to bed at half-past twelve.

The next day, 31st, orders to proceed to Lanz, and wait further orders. We got there about ten o'clock, and I turned my horses into the forage remaining in the French camp of the night before,

and got some collected for the mules. Thus we
remained loaded until four o'clock without orders.
Lord Wellington then sent on for fresh horses and
his light canteens, and of our own accord we unloaded to relieve the animals, but for a long time
durst not unpack. At last, General Murray came
in, and ordered some dinner; but saying he had
no authority to direct others to do the same. This
put others in motion, however, and, amongst them,
Mr. Haines. We were all to go to our old quarters; but, not liking in this state of things to go
over to Arriez, my old place, where I had lost myself in the night, I got a room at Haines's, and
some dinner, hung my baggage cover up for a
door, and went to sleep on the table to avoid the
fleas

The next day, 1st of August. about six o'clock,
orders were issued to advance to Berrueta, and
there to remain, waiting orders again. We returned over this mountain thus the third time, and
got to Berrueta about one o'clock. I called at
Almendoz as I passed, to remind the patrona of
the house that I had told her we should beat the
French, near Pamplona, and be back in a week. I
was so in five days, and found her more miserable
than before from the plunder by the French. I
gave the green Indian corn the French had left to

my horse, and wished her good-bye. About two
o'clock, we heard that we had driven the French
off the hills above St. Estevan and also through
the town, and head-quarters were to move on to
St. Estevan directly. We did so, and got there by
five o'clock; the French having been driven out
between twelve and one. We saw about a dozen
French, just killed, close to St. Estevan, but got
comfortable quarters, and went to dinner. So we
go on, you see!

The French being driven in, about two leagues
towards Lezaca and Echalar, Longa and the
Spaniards, and the light division, made a long
march back that day, the 1st of August, towards
their own ground above Lezaca, going more round,
however, towards Echalar. By this, the 95th fell
in with the French at the bridge, where the road
to Lezaca divides from that to Echalar, headed
them, killed and wounded about a hundred, and,
without discovering it, before dark, drove much of
their baggage up the valley round again towards
St. Estevan. By this movement, the French being
then headed at the Lezaca valley, went the
Echalar pass and road instead, and in confusion;
and the baggage walked into the fourth division
just as they advanced the next morning.

Yesterday, the 2nd of August, our orders were

to proceed to this place, our old place, Lezaca. We started, and got into all the baggage of head-quarters—three divisions—eight miles extent of loaded mules in a string. There was a halt of about four hours, and no one could move ; this was until we got near where the baggage had been caught, and I believe this was the cause. After fighting by all the baggage, and leading my horse along some very dangerous places, where, if he slipped, he went down to the river—from four to five mules actually did—I got to this baggage scene, and then went quietly on. For nearly two miles, there were scattered along the road, papers, old rugs, blankets, pack-saddles, old bridles, girths, private letters, lint, bandages, boxes, one or two hundred, empty and broken; quantities of in-trenching tools, rags, French clothes, dead mules, dead soldiers and peasants, farriers' tools, officers' boots, linen, &c. There were also the boxes of M. Le General Baron de St. Pol, and several private officers' baggage ; but the principal thing taken seemed to be the *ambulance du 2ème divi-sion ;* that is, the field hospital of the second divi-sion. There were still more things worth picking up, and some soldiers digging up three live mules out of an old limekiln near the road-side, and this caused stoppages and confusion.

Just beyond the bridge of Yanza were the French, wounded by the 95th the night before, crawling off; and we twice met small parties of prisoners going to the rear, abused not a little by the plundered and exasperated villagers. The prisoners told me the country people about these mountains were *"diablement méchant,"* and treated them very ill. The truth was, however, that the French began ; for though they had behaved well in the advance, they had plundered and destroyed considerably in their retreat, and much wantonly. I told them they ought never to have come and entered Spain, to which they replied, " We never wished to do so ; it is not our fault."

About three o'clock, I went round to see what was going on, but my horse was tired, and I could not get up the hill to see the French driven from the hill above Echalar, and also from the light division hill. In short, all our old position, and a little more, was gained last night. I got nothing to eat until near nine o'clock, as baggage was so late, and I am not sorry for to-day's halt, I assure you.

In our advance again, we also saw some of the effects of our own retreat. In one place, there was an ammunition waggon, with six dead mules, which had all rolled down the mountain together.

I ascertained it to be English by sending a muleteer down for some papers in the waggon, which
turned out to be our printed blank artillery returns.
I also saw four other wheels and parts of carriages,
and I believe we lost a howitzer. Colonel Ross's
troop suffered, I believe, the most in this way.
The French seem to have made this as a desperate
push to relieve Pamplona and St. Sebastian. The
garrisons both sallied; that of Pamplona was
driven back directly, as I hear; that of St. Sebastian (as we are told) surprised us in the trenches
napping, as the heavy guns were all embarked for
security, and nothing going on, and carried off
three companies of Portuguese. I hope this is exaggerated. Near Elisondo, I hear, we took thirty
cars of bread and brandy, and some baggage also—
a day's bread for two divisions; and many now
are fighting without it on both sides. There is no
delivery of bread to-day, even for head-quarters;
corn for the horses we have had none this week.

Head-quarters have stray papers to the 19th,
which I am reading whilst the fighting is going on.
One great amusement in these papers, to me at
least, is the excess of lies, the impudence, the
abundance of them, and then the blunders, and
ignorance of what is going on. You will be surprised at the contents of this, when you get the

Gazette account, as you will long first probably.
I told you, I remember, the beaten army would
return in a month; whether they will muster
again this year, and attack, depends, I think, upon
the fall of Pamplona and St. Sebastian, and the
northern war.   Pamplona is, I hope, starving; at
least without meat; but I still doubt, except that
this sudden effort proves danger.   It is merely
more closely invested by small gun redoubts—no
battering gun has ever been near it, at present
only about six thousand Spaniards watch it, and I
think if they choose they might be off, only much
harassed by our cavalry, &c.

Your Life Guard charges were the most ludicrous.
They were never near the enemy, until beyond
Vittoria, as I was before them and almost run
down twice by their anxiety along the road, gal-
loping away without occasion.   I leaped a ditch
once to avoid them, not wishing to blow my horse
as theirs were, at a time when we were on one side
of Vittoria and the French on the other.   They
were afterwards ordered on, but never came up
with the enemy, and could do nothing in such a
country, with six-foot ditches round the inclosures.
Very few of the Spaniards have behaved well this
time.   They have been generally in the rear; one
regiment stood fire well on the 28th but some ran,

and in general I hear they have done little.
Longa's people tolerably here. There has been
sharp work on the whole. I should put the allied
losses at six thousand, or *in toto* seven thousand,
and the French at eighteen thousand nearly, provisions and all, that is somehow put *hors de
combat*. If the Spaniards will not fight, we can
scarcely stand even this advantage long; we shall
be ruined by our victories. The French under
d'Erlon behaved very well to Colonel Fenwick,
who was left wounded; no one was allowed to go
to his house as a quarter, and every attention was
paid both to him and the surgeon left with him. The
latter became so popular that the French liked to be
dressed by him, better than by their own surgeons.

August 3rd, six o'clock, evening.—The great
men are all come in; and I am told nothing has been
done more to-day. The last push over the hills,
and out of their position has not been made yet.
So at least says General O'Lalor. I suspect the
Prince of Orange will carry home these despatches,
and I think it but fair now, that he should go and
see his intended as a conquering hero. He certainly promises very well. I have an old man,
just returned home, thrashing out his wheat over
my head, thus employed all the morning, giving
me his dust as well as his noise.

Later, nine o'clock evening.—Nothing has been done to-day; and the French remain nearly in their strong ground above. Bera, a league and a half from this. It was found, I believe, necessary to turn it regularly to avoid great loss, for though one brigade of red coats yesterday turned two French divisions off one high hill, we can scarcely expect this always. I think, therefore, we shall remain here some days at least. I have just heard an anecdote of General Picton. General Cole on the 17th ordered General Byng to retire from a post on a hill which afterwards formed a part of our good position on the 28th. Byng sent to Picton to say what his orders were, and added that though very important, he felt he was not strong enough to justify his keeping it. Picton said to Byng's aide-de-camp, " No, by G— he shall not give up the hill, I will bring my division up to support him ; but no, your horse is done up. I'll go myself and tell him ;" and he ordered the division to follow—this saved that hill. Another time, General Cole was by orders leaving a hill, when he had fresh orders to occupy it. His men found a few stragglers on the top, and the French main division half way up. They gave them such a volley and warm reception, that they soon turned back and were off.

We were very nearly destroying some of the French cavalry, and taking two divisions. Two things prevented this. The night we were at Berrueta two of our fellows straggled, and got taken, and they told the French where head-quarters were. This made them conclude we were strongly posted close by, and they decamped at night instead of the morning, as they had intended. Thus several hours were gained. The next thing was—our light division got their orders seven hours later than was expected. Had they been that time sooner up, they would have headed the French division on their road to Echalar, as well as to Lezaca, and from strong ground might have been able to drive them back upon the other divisions and have surrounded them. Their cavalry also would have been caught on this narrow winding road down by the river, where the baggage was destroyed, with a path in the wood just on the opposite side, from whence our fellows might at least have picked off the horses if the men chose to run away. This was just missed, however, from these causes, and remains one of the *ifs* and *ands ;* it is very provoking, as that would have completely crippled them for this year.

A Spanish priest told me to-day that all the priests, nuns, &c. in Spain, were constantly putting up prayers for Lord Wellington, thinking almost everything depended upon him individually, as I believe most people here do think. They were sorry he was so often exposed as he is to fire.

Lezaca, August 4th, 1813.—Nothing to be done, I believe, to-day. Everything in *statu quo;* the Prince goes to-night or to-morrow morning with despatches to England, and I shall send this with them.

P.S. It feels, as you may suppose, very strange, after the whirl about to Pamplona and all the scenes I have witnessed, to be again quietly drawing charges at Lezaca; but so it is, and I have only lost a frying-pan and a pair of stockings in the confusion. I have just heard that the French have increased their force much in our front above Bera on their hills, and I think nothing more will be done immediately on our part or on theirs.

CHAPTER II.

REJOICINGS FOR THE VICTORY—SUFFERINGS OF COLE'S DIVI-
SION—COMPLAINTS OF THE FRENCH—STATEMENTS OF A
FRENCH PRISONER—DECAY OF SPAIN—CHARACTERISTICS
OF WELLINGTON — HIS OPINION OF BONAPARTE — PROS-
PECTS OF A RENEWAL OF THE ATTACK—EXCHANGE OF
PRISONERS—WELLINGTON'S SPANISH ESTATE—HIS OPINION
OF PICTON—DISPOSITION OF THE ARMY.

Head Quarters, Lezaca,
August 7, 1813.

MY DEAR M——,

HERE we are still, quiet and *in statu quo
ante* our last run to Pamplona. I have sent you a
long account of all this business with the Prince of
Orange's despatches.

Our cavalry have been moving up, both to St.
Estevan and towards Irun. From the former place,
however, for want of forage they begin to retire
again. Much are left still round Pamplona, where
there is only a Spanish infantry force to watch
and invest. They have tried in vain to burn the
corn just under the walls of the town, and this
supplies the garrison partly. Marshal Beresford

is gone for a week to the sea side, for bathing; I conclude, therefore, nothing is to be immediately undertaken to turn the French out of the remaining hills near here. I should like to have them clear out in the plains below, as I expect in about three weeks to have them plaguing us again; otherwise, I think something is still in agitation for this purpose, but for the present delayed. We fired, at St. Sebastian, a salute of twenty-one guns for our late victory. The garrison regularly returned two for every gun fired. They are very well supplied, it is said, and are very impudent. I fear all our former breaches will now be quite useless, as they are probably, ere this, made the strongest points. Saragossa, or Zaragoza (the fort there I mean) has surrendered to Mina with about forty guns, and I hear nearly five hundred men ; this will be good, if Suchet intends to come that way towards us. I think he is now retreating a little, and perhaps this late business may make him go back quicker.

Lord Wellington was on his bed yesterday, and could scarcely rise from the lumbago ; but was in good humour and good spirits. His position near Sosavren and Orcayen, or Orquin, was a near-run thing, (this was where the last two battles were fought). General Cole was there with the fourth division. In the course of his retreat, Lord Wellington was falling back on him with his staff, saw the importance of the position and galloped over the bridge, and up to General Cole, to form his division, and take up the position at first sight. Pamplona must otherwise have been relieved, and the French were so close upon Lord Wellington, that a part of his staff rather behind could not follow him over the bridge, but were cut off by the French, and obliged to find their way round. This position was afterwards strengthened by the third (Picton's) division, and the Spaniards, and this at least saved the communication with Pamplona. I hope we should in any case have beaten the French at last, but it must have been further back certainly, and probably I think on the Tolosa road. General Cole's division has had, on the whole, nearly nine days' constant fighting and marching. It is terribly cut up in consequence.

The French vow vengeance against the Spaniards. An officer, prisoner here, told me yesterday, the Spaniards had always complained of them, the French, and often with reason ; but if they came again as he expected, the French were resolved to show them the difference, and let them have some reason to complain of them in earnest He said, France had lost nearly four hundred thousand men in Spain, in the war, and above half by far from sickness and unfair means, assassination and treachery. He said there was not a family in France that had not put on mourning for this Spanish war, and yet scarcely any of the Spaniards had fought them like men. He said the notion the French had was that in the general peace which was expected, England and France would make arrangements to divide the best part of Spain between them, and that we should keep Cadiz, Carthagena, and all the useful maritime parts, and leave them to the Ebro. He smiled much at my disowning any such honest and honourable intentions on our part. He told me the French armies had suffered more in their *morale* here, in the last campaign, than by their Russian losses, as every Frenchman laid the latter entirely to climate, and was satisfied he still could conquer a Russian as formerly; but here, the troops were fairly beaten, and in general would not stand. Only two brigades, he said, behaved really well at Vittoria, and Jourdan was sent to Paris under arrest for his conduct. As to the money, baggage, &c., they behaved much better on the 18th of July.

He also told me that even an English or Spanish officer in the best of times had never been so well treated as the French were when they first came here. He appeared not at all to feel how much worse this made their conduct since. It was drawn out by my telling him that Bonaparte had contrived now to make the French detested, almost by every nation in Europe, and power was all he had to rely upon. The part Bernadotte had taken the French officers seem not to have known, so much are they kept in the dark about every thing.

My Frenchman also said, that had it not been for the jealousies of the Guerillas, they might by acting in concert (which they never would do) have sometimes almost annihilated whole French divisions, and that the French could scarcely have kept their ground some time since; but by local jealousies, and individual jealousies, the finest opportunities were lost. He said the good or bad behaviour of an army all depended on pay and food, or the contrary, want of both, and I believe this much, and that he rightly said that the French discipline was the best when they had both, but that not being here ever the case, plunder, &c., was the consequence. "But why come here at all?" quoth I, "*L'Empereur le veut,*" was the answer, "and we as soldiers have only to obey." "Try and enter France," he said, "and you will soon see how the people feel, and whether your stories of a readiness to revolt, and dissatisfaction are true. So far from it, that there has been considerable zeal shown every where in replacing the Emperor's Russian losses." The French think there must be war, and therefore the further from home the better. We have heard before you, by French papers, of the extension of the armistice in the North. This is bad for the campaign here.

The man who was tried for a rape the day before our last rumpus begun, was found guilty, was kept safe all through the confusion, and was to have been executed yesterday near the place at Urday, when he contrived over night to escape. If the French knew his excuse for this offence, that he thought he was in France, he would not be very well received by them. I am now enquiring who are alive in my other cases which were disturbed.

The English reviewers and others may say what they please as to Spain not having been on the decline during the last century. It has at least stood still when almost every other country in Europe has made rapid advances in everything. In Spain and Portugal, no town is now, or has been lately, on the increase—several manifestly diminished. The decay of houses is seldom made good, even on the same ground, by new ones; I do not suppose I have in the whole country seen four new houses building in spite of the thousands

destroyed of late, nor does this seem owing to the
last five years and the times at present, as you see
no houses commenced before that time, and left
unfinished by that event, at least extremely few.
In France, almost every large place had its new
town as in England, only in a less degree, and
evident marks of new buildings, &c., stopped by
the Revolution. In Spain there are no appearances of new towns at all, nor of parts of towns,
or scarcely even houses, or unfinished buildings
stopped by the present confusion—some in Vittoria, from French excitement I believe, but
nothing to speak of. The churches are every
where on a large and expensive scale, and a few
modern, but in general old. The Spanish towns
have nearly all the appearance of what we should
take to be decayed manufacturing towns. The
inhabitants appear to have been asleep as to the
rest of the world, and not to have made any progress whilst others made great advances. This is
a sort of decline. There can have been little
demand for manufactures, as the same few chairs
and tables seem to have been in use these fifty or
hundred years. White-washing and new placing
the tiles seem the only repairs of the houses.

Yet, I think many districts seem to have been
uncommonly happy and comfortable before this

war—large tight houses, abundance of food, good clothes, cleanly habits, a general equality of rank ; no rich among them at all, no very poor ; and no manufactures. Every man almost could make what he wanted for his farm, and a shoemaker, a tailor, and a farrier nearly the only tradesmen, except farmers, in work. Occasional pedlars supplied the other wants of a people who had but few. Such must have been the independent, happy state of many large districts away from the influence of the corruptions of the large towns, where all the idle, lazy, pauper nobility lived, and alike free from the effects of the misgovernment and oppressive conduct of their rulers. Other districts certainly were very different, and more like the dirty and ill-provided Portuguese. In Portugal, the higher classes seem, I think, to have been generally better off, and to have enjoyed themselves more in their quintas, or villas, and the poor to have been worse off. There are none of the districts in Portugal such as I have described in Spain.

I have just met General Cole, who commanded the fourth division ; he is quite knocked up ; he says, his division only have one hundred and four officers killed and wounded.

Lezaca, 8th August.—I dined yesterday solus

early, and rode up to the hill at the point of our
position above Bera, from whence you see Bayonne,
&c., &c. I stood on the top until near dark, and
returned down the mountains by moonlight. The
French fires were very numerous, and burnt all
over the sides of a tremendous hill, which they
still occupy opposite to our position. I passed the
boundary stone, and got half-a-mile into France, to
the highest summit of our rock, where the out-
lying picket is. I saw the French relieve their
pickets, heard their drums as plain as ours, saw
the men at work at a redoubt to oppose us if we
advanced, and, lastly, saw five thousand Spaniards
come to occupy the ground in the place of our
light division, &c., who were to go elsewhere.
These were O'Donnell's regiments ; they were thin
in numbers. A brigade, nominally three thousand,
mustered one thousand eight hundred, but were
well-dressed and good-looking men. I only hope
they will fight—at least that they do not steal as
adroitly as Longa's people ; we have had the
latter near here, and nothing is safe at all from
their fingers from a horse or mule down to a bit of
biscuit. You will see, in my Vittoria letter I think
it was, that I told you the Frenchmen as an army
had escaped, and that we should hear of them

again in a month. So it was ; and so I think it will be probably again, unless the two places surrender to us in a few weeks.

This small, verminy, dirty place, Lezaca, is a curious scene of bustle just now ; crowded with Spanish fugitives—the head-quarters no small body, with all our stragglers and Longa's, who are more numerous (he having a quarter here now, and looking like an English butcher in a handsome hussar dress), with abundance of Spanish and Portuguese officers (as both troops are near), as well as with English, with passing wounded and prisoners, with mules and muleteers innumerable, besides all the country people who come here to turn all they have got into money; noises of all sorts ; thrashing all going on in the rooms up stairs ; the corn then made into bread and sold in one corner ; "*aqua ardente*" crying all about ; lemonade (that is, dirty water and dark brown sugar) the same ; here a large pig killing in the street, with its usual music on such occasions ; another near it with a straw fire singeing it, and then a number of women cutting up and selling pieces of other pigs killed a few hours before ; suttlers and natives with their Don Quixotte wineskins all about, large pigskins, and small ditto, and middling ditto, all pouring out wine to our half-boozy, weary soldiers ;

bad apples and pears, gourds for soup, sour plums, &c., all selling at once. Perpetual quarrels take place about payment for all these things between the soldiers of the three allied nations and the avaricious and unreasonable civilian natives; mostly, however, between Spaniards and Spaniards. The animals eating green Indian corn almost against every house here and in the churchyard, which contains four tents all from the same cause, want of stables, &c., of quarters; and not the least curious or noisy in this confusion, about fifteen men and women with fresh butter 4s. the pound, who are come from near St. Andero and beyond it, —a stout race dressed in a curious, peculiar manner —and who contrive to bring butter on their heads in baskets for above a fortnight together, and sell it at last in a state that I am very glad to eat it for breakfast for ten days after it arrives. It forms a sort of very mild cream cheese, in fact.

Head-Quarters, Lezaca, August 9th.—You ask me if Lord Wellington has recollected —— with regard? He seems to have had a great opinion of him, but scarcely has ever mentioned him to me. In truth, I think Lord Wellington has an active, busy mind, always looking to the future, and is so used to lose a useful man, that as soon as gone he seldom thinks more of him. He would be always, I have no doubt, ready to serve any one who had been about him who was gone, or the friend of a deceased friend, but he seems not to think much about you when once out of the way. He has too much of everything and everybody always in his way to think much of the absent. He said the other day, he had great advantages now over every other General. He could do what others dare not attempt, and he had got the confidence of all the three allied powers, so that what he said or ordered was, right or wrong, always thought right. " And the same" (said he) " with the troops ; when I come myself, the soldiers think what they have to do the most important as I am there, and that all will depend on their exertions ; of course, these are increased in proportion, and they will do for me what perhaps no one else can make them do."   He said, he had several of the advantages possessed by Bonaparte, from his freedom of action and power of risking, without being constantly called to account ; Bonaparte was quite free from all inquiry, he was himself in fact very much so. The other advantages Bonaparte possessed, and which he made so much use of (Lord Wellington said) was his full latitude of lying ; *that,* if so disposed, he said, he could not do.

You ask about health — I think this hole in the

mountains unwholesome; the place is so full, and stinking; the air heavy and oppressive; it is like Devonshire, warm moisture constantly. I long to be on the mountains, to get air, and braced up. It has rained nearly all the last twenty-four hours.

August 10*th.*—I have just seen Lord Wellington, about some more than usually important business; he is better, but not well. He has given me an immense bundle of English and Spanish papers to peruse and examine.' The enclosed plan may help you a little to understand the *Gazette*, and my letter, remember it is only my hasty personal sketch in pen and ink, on no scale, and taken from no regular document.

11*th, Post-day.*—I worked very hard all yesterday, and could not get through Lord Wellington's papers. I am still at work at the last part: a Spanish narrative of all the Spanish operations of a Spanish army for a month, by their General, Copons. It consists of sixty-four sides of foolscap in a Spanish hand. I therefore have not time for more. There is nothing new. Lord Wellington gives a dinner to-morrow, in honour of the Prince Regent's birth-day, to all the heads of departments, to which I go. There are reports of the French moving already, but I believe all lies as yet. Do not be too sanguine about Suchet. He may retire, but will hardly be forced out of the country, as there are forty thousand French on that side of Spain. The Spanish government have given Lord Wellington a handsome royal estate near Granada; he told me this yesterday.

Head-quarters, Lezaca, August 13, 1813.— Here I am, and very busy still, and with no events to communicate. All now is quiet for the present, as at Frenada, though this cannot last long. Having the paper by me, however, I determined to place this letter upon the stocks, against the next post-day.

I dined yesterday at Lord Wellington's, with a party of thirty-six, to keep the Prince Regent's birthday; eight mules had arrived in the morning with prog, and wines, from Bilbao, and we had, therefore, a good feast, and some very good claret of Majoribanks and Paxton. Our party was but very dull, though many grandees :—Castanos, O'Donnell, the General of the army of the reserve (the best Spaniards I have seen, and now on the hill above us, with something like a Commissariat, &c.), their Aide-de-camps, &c., Generals Cole, Anson, Murray, Pakenham, &c., &c. There were two bands of the Fusileers, and the 7th; and Fuento, the Spanish Commissary, gave us " God

2 D

save the King," and Lord Wellington's favourite,
" Ah Marmont, onde Va Marmont ?" but it was
very hot and stupid ; every one here is fagged, and
half done up.   Lord Wellington could scarcely rise
when he sat down, or sit down when he rose, from
the lumbago, and was in great pain, but is
much better ; all around him look pale and worn.
I think, however, we shall be up to another brush
again soon.

We are about to begin again soon at St. Sebastian ; but I fear it will be hard and bloody work,
unless some piece of good luck should arise in our
favour.

Later.—I have just been to Lord Wellington,
with the result of my labours, which have amused
him much, and which he thinks I cannot be correct
in, as to facts, or if so, the whole, he agrees, is most
extraordinary ; and he has now got the papers, and
my statement, to examine.   I can only say, it is
not, I think, the Spanish General who was to
blame ; I must not explain more at present ; he
seemed pleased, as he asked me to dinner again to
day.   We have a stray paper to the 4th, which has
set us all agog ; but I have only heard the news
concerning Lord Aberdeen, and it does not seem
quite certain that there is to be an ambassador from
England to the congress.   The French nation, or

rather the news through France, is, I hear, all for peace, and that the Rhine and the Pyrenees are to be the boundaries, Jerome King of Holland, and Joseph King of Italy ; this is only French rumour.

I am told, that Soult says he will be here the day after to-morrow, the 15th, and has two bridges ready near Irun, to come on our left ; I wish he would come there, as I think we should be able to do something then, as we are well up for an attack there ; four hours would put the divisions here on that flank, Spaniards, &c.

The 14*th.*—A little more leisure, so I proceed. We had last night a little firing, but I believe it was only the Spaniards. The latter and the French fire at each other every opportunity, and when neighbours, are never at peace. Our sentries and the French are within one hundred yards of each other, and relieved regularly without the least molestation on either side. This is the true thing. Unless an attack is to be made, what is gained by killing a poor sentry ? Our new brigade is not yet at Passages, though expected this fortnight. Some reinforcements are, however, come up, and the sick brigade of Guards, which were left behind, have, by easy marches from Oporto, now joined us ; about one thousand five hundred out of the three thousand who came out at that unlucky

time last year. The French have also reinforcements, and must in honour do something if the
two places hold out. The French gentleman who
came over to us near Pamplona fourteen days
since, dined at Lord Wellington's yesterday, and
talked away. He seems clever, and, like every
Frenchman, professed to know everything—the
secret history of everybody and of every event.
He calls Bonaparte *un tigre*, &c. &c. I cannot
say I like him much, and would not trust him : I
am not much afraid of Lord Wellington's doing
so. Lord Wellington told him concerning the
exchange of prisoners in this country. He said
Massena once agreed to exchange three hussar
officers and one hundred and twenty men, rank for
rank, and when he had got his own three officers
and the men, sent back only twenty soldiers, and
the rest countrymen and Portuguese militiamen,
and three officers of militia scarcely embodied.
Lord Wellington vowed never to trust his honour
again, and in every proposal always excepts Massena. Indeed he said he was so little inclined
now, from experience, to trust any of them, that a
short time since, when an exchange was proposed,
he said, " Yes ; but first name the officers and
men you offer, and their regiments, ages, &c., and
then I will treat, but I will not have Spanish pea-

sants for French soldiers." To this they sent no answer.

He also tells them, until our travellers, civilians, &c., who were detained are released, he can never listen to non-combatant pleas. All must be exchanged ; but he is very liberal. He also said Soult once complained that six of our officers had escaped from their guard near Oporto, on that retreat, and had committed a breach of honour, but that he (Lord Wellington) having inquired into it, found they were placed in confinement under a guard, and their parole not relied upon, and that they had got the better of their guard. Lord Wellington, therefore, told the Marshal that the parole being abandoned by the imprisonment, the point of honour was gone, and that there were two ways of prisoners and their guards separating, and that he believed the guard had run away from their prisoners, and not the prisoners from their guard. To this also he had no answer.

Lord Wellington also talked of Grant's case. who lately got away from Paris. Lord Wellington had advised him not to give his parole in Spain, and had provided persons to rescue him in several places on the march to France. They offered this to Grant in consequence, but the offer was from honour declined, as the parole had been given and acted upon. The moment he was in France the French placed him under a guard, and at Bayonne he got away from them and went to Paris, remained there nine months, and got to England at last. Lord Wellington yesterday was excessively stiff and sore, but in high spirits. He seems to have a notion that the Continent will make a peace, and leave us and the Spaniards in the lurch, and I believe this prevents any very forward movements here on his part, as the French would then soon come down upon us with decidedly superior numbers; and if we had quite passed these mountains a hasty retreat back through them would not be a very easy or agreeable manœuvre.

I rode last night to Bera or Vera, where our outposts are in the valley. The French pickets are in two houses on the hills opposite, a few hundred yards up. Several of the houses about there are destroyed, gutted, and burnt, and most of them deserted. It was, a month ago, a pretty little town. Longa had also, since we were here last, burnt two nice farms on the road there, and knocked off the parapet of the bridge, and dug a trench across for the purpose of annoying the French. We have headed nearly all the green Indian corn in this valley for the horses; it is cut short off, half way, leaving the fruit below; and this is said not to do much harm to the corn. But then we cannot eat our cake and have it also. There will be no dry forage for the animals in autumn and winter. The little wheat straw there is about these valleys is nearly all eaten already, and much of the wheat and Indian corn itself has been either destroyed or taken by the irregularity of the thousand muleteers around us, in spite of their being occasionally flogged for this when caught. The inhabitants will, I fear, be half starved in the winter, unless they migrate, which many will, I have no doubt, and we must be supplied from elsewhere if we stay near here. Spain in general will, however, have been released from the supply of, nominally, two hundred thousand French; and as we drove them before harvest time, most of this will be in the market somewhere, except what has been destroyed on our immediate line of march. Much has been of course trodden down, and from the want of forage and corn our horses have been obliged to take the ripe wheat and eat it, straw, grain, and all, to serve both purposes. This is dangerous food; and if drink is given carelessly, often kills the animal; but otherwise answers well.

We understand here that it was three days after the news of the battle of Vittoria arrived before

any one durst inform Bonaparte of it. I think he
will have this last business almost entirely concealed from him, which can be managed, perhaps,
as we are now both *in statu quo* as to place,
though he is about fifteen thousand men minus to
what he was before the attack at Maya began.
From intercepted letters we find that, in reports
even to each other, the French lie considerably, or
at least misrepresent, for the good of the service,
and this will be a good occasion, as Bonaparte is
so far off.

In this little town, or rather village, there are
about twelve priests at least, walking about with
their shovel hats. The latter would astonish the
most orthodox bishop's chaplain in England, and
our coalheaver's hat is nothing to them. The only
fine cloth in the shops here is black, you may guess
for whose use.

The estate which the Spanish government has
given to the Marquis of Wellington is, I understand, a very desirable one, and the best proof of
that is, that it was one which the Prince of Peace
had given to himself, and I have no doubt he chose
the best he could find. It is nominally thirty
thousand dollars a-year, a castle, I understand, and
about a league from Granada, in a fine country.
Lord Wellington seems very much pleased with it.

He says he hopes the house is a good one, as he should not like to have to build, and that he hears there is hunting, coursing, fishing, and everything near home. There was a fine wood, but I fear the Prince of Peace cut most of that down. General O'Lalor, who is in a bad state of health, is to have the government of Granada, and will super-intend this estate for Lord Wellington. The latter had got the papers concerning it before him when I called a few days since, and said, " This is about the estate they have given me."

The 15*th.*—I have been very ill all night and this morning, but am now rather better, and the doctor tells me I am thus saved a fever by this bilious attack, which is always something gained. We are all most anxious for news from the North, as all here must depend in the end upon it, in a great measure at least. Next to " General Frost," I think our General has done the most for the common cause. General Villa Alba, the Spanish Inspector of Cavalry, dined at head-quarters to-day. He is a queer-looking creature, in appearance like any-thing but a General, and much less a cavalry one. I know, however, nothing of his real character. We now feel the effects of our work through these valleys. We cannot ride a few miles without the alternate smells which succeed each other of dead

horses, dead mules, and dead men. A nice judge
can tell each by their particular *goût*, and that of
men is much the strongest. Bonaparte's birth-
day has passed very quietly, except a tremendous
triple salvo of all the St. Sebastian's guns and mortars upon our poor fellows in the trenches at daylight. The garrison are amazingly pert, from their
success hitherto. We have some hopes they will
soon want water. I am stupid, so for to-day
adieu.

The 16th.—Much the same to-day, attack continuing all night. Henry is also rather unwell, and
two of my Portuguese servants. I cannot think
what it is in this country that affects us. The
thermometer has never in the shade, in my room,
been beyond 72° in this part of Spain. General
Sir T. Picton is attacked again with a violent
bowel complaint, and is fallen to the rear. He
would be a great loss, as he is one of the best
here. Lord Wellington the other day said, " Why,
even General Picton did so-and-so the other day,"
as if surprised that he should not have acted quite
right.

Our soldiers are quite unaccountable; all is
going on right, and they are just now quiet and
well fed, and yet desertion, and even of British, to
the enemy, was scarcely ever more frequent. I

was not surprised at one hundred and forty of the
Chasseurs Britanniques going off when we were
falling back to Pamplona, and as they thought
probably to Portugal; but the English soldier deserting is astonishing and unaccountable. Three
went off from pickets together the other night,
towards the French, and were all caught, and to
be tried. Several must be hung for this. Two
new regiments are at last arrived. I wish the
French would come fairly on now, if at all, but
every one talks of a general peace. Adieu.

The 17*th.*—We have this day a strong French
report that peace is signed, and that the Pyrenees
are to be the boundary of France on this side;
" nothing said about England ;" but even, at this
rate, we must be off if this prove true. Your news
of the fifty thousand men, under Soult, you will
have seen was tolerably correct, and it was intended
he should have been here sooner, to prevent the
mischief which happened at Vittoria. As soon as
the report came that we were threatening to cross
the Ebro he was sent off, but he did not allow
sufficiently for Lord Wellington's rapid movements,
and was too late a little. It is clear, from many
circumstances, as Lord Wellington says, that he
intended to drive us back to the Ebro this last
push, and that his measures were all taken accord-

ingly: his cavalry, which he brought with him, and which for the country, as far as Pamplona, would have been useless, has suffered much from the roads, want of shoes, &c., and had no employment except carrying off the wounded.

Our army is now nearly thus: first and fifth divisions, Oyarsan and St. Sebastian, under Graham; Jeron, with his Spaniards of Gallicia, in their front at Irun; Longa between them and this place, with his diminished Guerillas; here the fourth division and the light in front, and the Spaniards of O'Donnell the reserve next, on the right of the others, in front; then the seventh division above Echallar, &c.; then the third and sixth in Maya and Roncesvalles Pass, with Spaniards I believe also, and General Hill's second division behind them in the valley of Bastan, Elisondo, &c.; six thousand Spaniards watching Pamplona, and our cavalry about there principally or in the rear of Graham.

The 18th, still Lezaca.—O'Donnell is unwell, from his wound in the leg, from which thirty splinters have been extracted: he is going to the baths. He is the Conde de Bispal, commanding the Army of Reserve. Jeron is to take his command now, and give up the Gallicians; our men, however, I am glad to learn, are in general considered as very healthy—General Cole told me his division particularly so—after all their fatigues. I believe the army have Lord Wellington to thank even for this principally. Last year the mules per company allowed by government were employed carrying the heavy iron camp-kettles, and our men had no tents, as, though allowed, they could not be carried ; this year Lord Wellington had light tin kettles made, one for every six men, for the mess, to be carried by one of the men, each having a small cooking machine of tin besides ; this plan sets the mules free and disposable, and thus three tents have been carried for every company, and allowing for absentees, guards, officers' servants, sentries, &c., this now nearly houses or covers all our men, and contributes much to the health of the army. It was entirely an arrangement of his own. The Portuguese are still without tents, as are the French and the Spaniards.

The French, however, are very expert at making wood huts, with fern on the top and for the bedding, tolerably comfortable except in heavy rains. So are now the Portuguese indeed, and many of them (as well as our men who happen not to have tent room) join two together, and giving up their blankets for sleeping on, make a good tent of them, which holds two very well, and only consists of their two muskets and two blankets, and now, since all our plunder, generally a good sack or piece of carpet at the rough weather side. Orders were given before we marched from Frenada by Lord Wellington to have all blankets looped and strengthened at the corners, for this purpose, all ready, as an excellent defence from the sun, even better than a tent, cooler, and a very tolerable one from rain.

I am rather better again to-day, and dine with General Cole, who is quartered here. My people in this house are up all night, making a noise, and baking for Longa, and all day the children are shaking the dirt and the fleas from above down upon me.

CHAPTER III.

REPORTED RENEWAL OF OPERATIONS AGAINST ST. SEBASTIAN—
EFFECTS OF THE WAR ON SPAIN AND PORTUGAL.—WELLING-
TON'S ACCOUNT OF RECENT PROCEEDINGS—COURTS MARTIAL
—PRISONERS SHOT—DISCUSSIONS ON WAR BETWEEN WEL-
LINGTON AND A FRENCH DESERTER—THE SIEGE RESUMED—
WORK OF THE HEAVY BATTERIES—TRIAL OF GENERAL
O'HALLORAN—VOLUNTEERS FOR THE STORMING PARTIES.

Head-Quarters, Lezaca,
August 21, 1813.

MY DEAR M——,

SEVERAL of our Vittoria sick and wounded
now begin to return and join their regiments.
Major Freemantle came back just in time for dinner
yesterday, to amuse us with all your madness in
England about Vittoria.

General Cole, with whom I told you I was going
to dine, lives very comfortably; to do this, even in
his way, he has now travelling with him about ten
or twelve goats for milk, a cow, and about thirty-
six sheep at least, with a shepherd, who always
march, feed on the road side, on the mountains,

&c., and camp with him. When you think of this, that wine and everything is to be carried about, from salt and pepper and tea-cups to saucepans, boilers, dishes, chairs, and tables, on mules, you may guess the trouble and expense of a good establishment here.

I mentioned to you the iron-works all about this country, and their simple construction. They make, I believe. excellent iron notwithstanding. For this purpose they mix the ore of this country, which is too brittle, with the ore they fetch from near Bilbao, which is rather too ductile and soft, and of the two form an excellent compound, which used to supply much of the southern part of France.

Our great guns are, I am told, to begin pounding to-day at St. Sebastian again, but I have not heard them yet. The old breach will not do at all ; it is, we are told, mined and filled with little intended explosions. A seventy-four and some frigates are now near. I wish they would let the sailors try the sea side when we storm. I think they would get in somehow at once into the castle.

August the 23*rd.*—I have been too busy to add a line since the last until now. I have now a fresh set of Courts in every division again, as my last are broken up. One Deputy Judge-Advocate sent me, out of curiosity, a history of his Court-casualties,

&c., nine members out of fifteen, and the Judge-Advocate, killed or severely wounded since the 22nd of May, two prosecutors and three witnesses, all officers. We are trying to clear as we go, and to prevent all arrears, and we hang away to prevent desertion. I am told the French do the same and still more, but their people will go to the rear home ; this is more natural. We are told ten men from each company are gone by orders to the rear also—some foolishly say to quell riots, for which purpose ten old men would be the most useless possible ; but the most plausible account is, to drill new conscripts. Some deserters say they are sent even to Italy for this ; I believe just now they are not prepared to move, and will be content to remain quiet. We have alternate accounts, of course, of war and peace. To-day two women, one French the other Spanish, of the French prisoners from Vittoria, came in here, on their way to join the French. Lord Wellington, however, has stopped them, and says he will have no more sent over until the French release about three hundred mothers and wives, &c., of the Guerillas, who were carried off by them as hostages for the return home of their Guerilla relations ; so they cry and think this very sad, to be put upon the same footing as such crea-tures. One of the ladies asked the Adjutant-

general whether she had better write to her friends
openly, to propose an exchange, or in cypher? Upon
which he thought a cypher lady should not remain
here at least long. We now give some flour to
Longa's people for bread, and try to make Regulars
of them.

It is very terrible that our people, muleteers,
soldiers, &c., do more mischief by far than the
French, except when the latter do it by way of
punishment and revenge; at ordinary times their
discipline is much better than ours. The heads of
the Indian corn are now nearly all eaten off about
here by the cattle, and cut by the soldiers to roast, as
well as the leaves for our animals. The Spaniards,
however, in some degree have their revenge; we
bring a quantity of money into the country in
spite of our bad pay, and this they fleece us out of
in high style. They sell everything like Jews,
and are naturally exorbitant, greedy, and avaricious; it seems the general character. So we go on!
They cheat our fellows as much as they can, and
our fellows get all they can gratis; upon the whole,
however, if stationary, we benefit the country I
believe.

Lord Wellington, yesterday, said it was stated in
his letters from Lisbon, that Portugal was miserable
without us. No money, no markets, nothing doing.

I believe he was half joking with the Portuguese agent here ; but really meant that we were much missed there. The muleteers with us are the worst. Their terms were, a dollar a-day each mule, and one for a man for every three mules, and rations. They have gone on four years, and more ; they are now, I believe, sixteen months in arrears in their pay, having just got one month lately. If paid up they would make fortunes, and have no pretence to behave ill. As it is, they steal, plunder, turn out their mules in the corn, &c., and from one of the most orderly classes in Spain, are become the least so. There are about ten thousand of the mules in this state, and I suppose four thousand muleteers. Their pay is more than the army almost ; and when is it to be paid or how ? there lies the rub.

I am a little better, but not well ; writing all day, with fleas up to the middle, from the floor, and all over me during the night. Flies biting and whizzing all round me from daylight to dark, just like a small grocer's country shop ; with the noise and dirt of six *paisanos* and five children, do not add to my comfort or recovery. The people say we have brought the plague of flies, and I believe we have increased it by the number of dead carcasses, and various kinds of filth caused by the density of our population at present. We do not bury as regularly as the French, either our offal or dead animals, or anything; the Spaniards not at all, unless we do it for them. To give you a notion of the flies, they eat up all my wafers, if left open, and spot my letters all over if left one day on the table.

Nothing can look in a higher state than the Portuguese troops. They are cleaner than our men; or look so, at least. They are better clothed now by far, as they have taken the best care of their clothes : they are much gayer, and have an air, and a *je ne scais quoi*, particularly the Caçadores both the officers and private men, quite new in a Portuguese. This is curious, to see the effects of good direction and example, how soon it tells. The French seem to do the same with Italians, and with every one ; or rather, have done so, for I hope this may now cease, in part at least.

Head-Quarters, Lezaca, 24th.—Having been writing nearly all day yesterday, I took an evening stroll, and then went and sat down on the churchyard parapet wall. In ten minutes who should come there but Lord Wellington, solus! After one turn, he came and sat on the wall with me, and talked for more than half an hour. Amongst other things I said, I hoped you in England would hear Soult's account of the Maya business first, as you then would be alarmed, and value the latter account by the Prince of Orange as it deserved.

He said " Why, at one time it was rather alarming, certainly, and it was a close-run thing. When I came to the bridge of Sahaugen, I saw the French on the hills, on one side, and was clear we could make a stand on the other hills in our position on the 28th ; but I found we could not keep Sahaugen, that it was exposed to their fire and not to ours. I determined to take the position, but was obliged to write my orders accordingly at Sahaugen, to send back instantly, as if they were not dispatched back directly the way I had come, I must have sent four leagues round in a quarter of an hour later. I stopped, therefore, to write accordingly, people saying to me all the time—'The French are coming !—The French are coming!' I looked pretty sharp after them, however, every now and then until I had done, and then set off, and I saw them just near one end of the village, as I went out at the other end ; and then we took our ground."

I then said, the only time I felt a little uneasy was, when we were stopped at Lanz, and sent across to Ligasso, as all the faces seemed very long, and the removal of the wounded was very much pressed.

This led him to explain more; and he said : " Had
I been as regularly informed of how matters stood
on the 26th and 27th, as I was of what had
passed on the 25th, that need not have happened;
but General Cole never told me exactly how far he
found it necessary to give way, or let me know by
what a superior force he was pressed, and that he
intended giving way, or my arrangements would
have been quite different ; and the French might
have been stopped sooner than they were. In truth,
I suspected all Soult's plan was only by manœuvres
to get me out of the hills, and to relieve one or
both places besieged, as things turned up, and succeeded for him, and I expected him to turn short
round towards St. Sebastian accordingly. I had
then no notion that with an army so lately beaten
he had serious thoughts, as I now am sure he had,
of driving us behind the Ebro. The consequence
was, the second division halted a day and a half
at Trinita and Berrueta, on the 26th, and till three
on the 27th ; and the seventh division only took a
short march to St. Estevan, as I was unwilling to
lose a bit more of the mountains than was absolutely necessary, from the probable loss of men in
recovering such ground. On the night before we
marched, or at three in the morning of the 26th, I
knew all that had passed on the first attack, and

acted accordingly. Had I been as well-informed, and had everything been communicated to me as punctually on the next evening, the march of several divisions would have been different. I should and could have pressed them more on the 27th ; there would not have been the risk and apparent alarm as to head-quarters, &c. ; and we should probably have stopped the French sooner. As it is, however, and as I had men who could fight, as the English did when they recovered the hill which had been lost, it has all ended very well."

We then got upon the expedition on the other side of the Peninsula ; and he explained some of the reasons for his instructions there. He was rather stiff with the lumbago ; but in high spirits. He said the Spanish generals thought the reason the French beat them was, that they had no good cavalry ; and that whenever they had our cavalry with them, they wanted to fight. This was what he was anxious to prevent, for, he said, our cavalry never gained a battle yet. When the infantry have beaten the French, then the cavalry, if they can act, make the whole complete, and do wonders ; but they never yet beat the French themselves.

Talking on this subject another day, Lord Wellington and all the officers present seemed to agree that a cavalry regiment did not know what real infantry fire was. They talk of a sharp carbine fire, which kills ten or twenty horses and half as many men ; but they could not exist ten minutes in a fire to which our infantry battalions are at times exposed ; they would be annihilated if they did not go threes about very quick indeed. Even in the infantry at times it was said, in less than half an hour, every mounted officer would be dismounted from his own or his horse's wounds, and perhaps not six men in a company out of sixty would remain.

Head-Quarters, Lezaca, August 25th.—We are as quiet here as at Frenada. Desertion is terrible. I think, however, Lord Wellington must stop it. We have only, as yet, tried five out of sixteen on trial : they are all sentenced to death, and all shot ! This will, I think, at least have a good effect on our new reinforcements. One of our officers did an odd thing to stop it ; and it answered, or has so hitherto ; he called his men together and addressing them said, " I want no men who wish to go to the French, and if any now will say they wish to go, I promise to send them in with a flag of truce." No one stirred, nor has any one stirred since ; but as to the legality of this plan there may be a query ?

Our great guns have now just begun pounding again at St. Sebastian ; we are to demolish everything this time; but still I fear we shall scarcely get in easily at last.

As to Pamplona, the reports are that they are now on half-rations, and have enough at that rate to last till the 15th of next month. It is provoking how much they have picked up. They have tried to send out another batch of inhabitants; but these have been sent in again to help eat; a hard fate to be made a mere tool for starvation! and I conclude they will not have the best commons even Pamplona can afford.

Head-Quarters, Lezaca, August 28th, 1813.— Here we are still quiet, and very busy; Court-martials all at work, &c. In these hills, however, our Provosts are not the most secure; and common precautions will not do against men who know they are probably to be shot in a day or two. I told you previously of a man who was to have been hung the next day, but who escaped overnight. Another Court is just cut short for the same cause. They adjourned till yesterday morning, for a witness for the prisoner, and in the night he was off. Another man under sentence of death near Maya, and three other deserters just taken as they were going over to the French, were put foolishly under the care of a man and a lad armed to convoy them a little way. They rose on them, took away their arms, and went over with them to the French post. I am sorry to say, however, we have still enough to hang.

The French deserter, the talkative Lieutenant-colonel, is here again, and has one great merit — he induces Lord Wellington to talk and discuss his old battles, &c., when this man was on the other side. Thus from the two I pick up a little of the cause of things, &c. Yesterday the conversation turned upon the retreat of the last year. The Frenchman said all their officers blamed Soult for his conduct after crossing the Tormes; that he was in fact nearer Rodrigo than our army, and might and ought to have cut us off, if he had pushed on. Lord Wellington observed, "I fully expected to find him on the high road; and I ordered nothing at all that way in consequence on the first day; afterwards, when I found he was not there, I took to it." The French officer replied, "From the rain and hazy weather, and bad roads, Soult was puzzled and afraid—he did not in the least know the English plans. He heard of some troops, and did not know whether they were a rear-guard or the main army, and so on; but when he found your Lordship making a stand collected at St. Munos, he said, '*Ah, que j'avois tort.*'" He then tried to pump Lord Wellington, and said, "If he had cut you off, perhaps you would have recrossed the Tormes, and made for the Benevente road? but you would have suffered much." Upon which Lord Wellington observed, "No, I certainly should have done no such thing; that would have been ruin. But, if you must know what I should have done, I should have done that which many thought I ought to have done as it was—I should have fought, and trusted to the bravery of my troops to get me out of the scrape." The Frenchman then said, "No one ought to have blamed you for not doing that, unless it were absolutely necessary, for the French were twenty thousand stronger than you were, and their cavalry was then very numerous, and in the highest order."

These conversations give a value to the Frenchman which he does not otherwise possess, though a clever man. I found Lord Wellington the day before yesterday busy with all the Spanish staff and General Murray, with a dozen great Spanish drawings and plans of the mountains about them; they were comparing our several labours together. The Spanish staff draughtsmen have a good character— I should have liked to have been called in, but I was only waiting an audience at the other end of the room.

Yesterday, Lord Wellington went off on horse-

back over the mountain for Irun; he then went on
to St. Sebastian, and was not back here till nearly
nine at night. They are pounding away at that
fortress from fifty-one pieces of ordnance, mortars
and all; but nothing is done yet.

The 29*th.*—No news yet. Still battering away
at St. Sebastian. We had a ridiculous event here
yesterday: an enraged bull, belonging, I believe,
to the Commissariat, broke into the quarters of
the Commissary-general, Sir Robert Kennedy, and
contriving to get to the room of the clerks, put all
to flight, one this way, the other that, in the
greatest alarm—all were dispersed in an instant.
After upsetting a few things, the bull retreated
into the garden, and jumped over the wall, without doing any serious mischief. The joke was,
that the owner had contrived this, on account of
non-payment.

Our fifty-one battering pieces have now been at
work three days, and have laid open one end of
the entire wall of the town of St. Sebastian, and
to-morrow is talked of for the assault. Two days
since the garrison made another sortie, and carried
off a few men; and, upon the whole, I think
people are not quite satisfied with the conduct of
the fifth division, who are employed. Ever since
our retreat and the former sortie, they seem to

have had in some measure a sort of panic. We have had a general Court-martial on Major O'Halloran, for neglect on that occasion as field-officer in the trenches; but he is acquitted on the ground that the orders he gave were correct, but that he was disobeyed. The facts on the trial were these :—

A sortie was expected all the night, and peculiar precautions were taken accordingly ; every fifth man, sentry, &c., by order of the General. All was quiet until an hour after day-break and more ; then a Captain Canvers, of Portuguese service, who has since shot himself, seems to have suffered the sentries to enter the trenches, and rest on their arms for security, without orders, or rather against orders. At a little after six out came the French, and another Portuguese captain seems to have misunderstood his orders, and did not let his sentries fire instantly, thinking that he had no orders to this effect ; he was made prisoner. In short, the consequence was, that about fifty French were in an instant in the trenches, when half-a-dozen of our people fired and fell back. The Portuguese were mostly in a panic, and they were nearly six hundred out of seven hundred then employed. They did once attempt to get up the bank and form, but the sandy ground gave way, and in they

went again. This increased the confusion, and no
exertions of our or their officers could rally the
men, until they had been quite driven out of the
trenches, and pursued to the little village in ruins
under the convent. There Major O'Halloran rallied
them, and, with a fresh English working party just
arrived, drove the French back again to the town,
but in the mean time many prisoners were made.

Lord Wellington, himself, I think, is not pleased
with the fifth division ; and, as some proof of this,
has ordered three hundred of the first division,
one hundred and fifty of the light, one hundred
and fifty of the fourth, and, I believe, one hundred
and fifty of the third (of each of which one-third
are to be of the Portuguese regiments), to march
to-day to assist in forming the storming-party to-
morrow. This is a cut at the fifth; and these men
are all volunteers, and the orders are to send men
who, by their cool courage and good conduct, will
be likely to succeed. In a measure the success of
this will depend on these qualities. The fifth division ought now to volunteer, trying first alone, I
think.

There was nothing but confusion in the two
divisions here last night (the light and fourth),
from the eagerness of the officers to volunteer, and
the difficulty of determining who were to be re-

fused and who allowed to go and run their heads into a hole in the wall, full of fire and danger! Major Napier was here quite in misery, because, though he had volunteered first, Lieutenant-colonel Hunt of the 52nd, his superior officer, insisted on his right to go. The latter said that Napier had been in the breach at Badajoz, and he had a fair claim to go now. So it is among the sub-alterns; ten have volunteered where two are to be accepted. Hunt, being Lieutenant-colonel, has nothing but honour to look to; as to promotion, he is past that. The men say they don't know what they are to do; but they are ready to go any-where.

I fear we shall find the French have run across a ditch and a new second wall behind those we have destroyed, and that we may have tough work yet. The shells, however, which are sent every ten minutes into the castle, and shake the dust out of its roof in a fine style, must make the place rather warm to hold just now; and I heartily wish it would induce them to give in before all the bloodshed begins. They fire now but very little. Lord Wellington and every one is gone over to St. Sebastian to-day, and, having nothing to do, I have made up my mind to be off also.

August 30th.—I was on the point of setting out

when I heard that the storming was put off a day;
as the French are in motion, and making pretence at least to relieve St. Sebastian, and as the
fourth division marched accordingly this morning,
and head-quarters may, therefore, suddenly be off,
I determined to be quiet here, especially as I do
not feel quite well.   Lord Wellington came home
at nine o'clock, and was off again before eight this
morning.   We remain here much in the dark, of
course, when he is away.   General Murray stays
here to protect us with the light division in our
front.

20th September, Mont de Marsan.—Alas, poor
Seymour!—[Hiatus.]   *   *   *

CHAPTER IV.

THE AUTHOR TAKEN PRISONER—KIND TREATMENT BY THE
FRENCH GENERAL—LIFE OF A PRISONER—RELEASE—DE-
TAILS OF THE AUTHOR'S CAPTIVITY — CURIOUS SCENE AT
GENERAL PAKENHAM'S—A BASQUE SQUIRE.

Bayonne, September 5, 1813.

MY DEAR M——,

WHEN you told me, some time since, that
you expected to hear from me from this place, I
never expected to have realised in this way your
prediction. But as the French all tell me with a
shrug, "*c'est le sort de la guerre, Monsieur*," I
must submit to as great a piece of ill-luck as generally falls to a poor man, "*dans le meilleur de
monde possible.*"

On the evening of the 30th August I was, as
I mentioned to you in my last, stopped from going
over to see the storming of St. Sebastian the next
morning by the general report that the French
were in motion; that an attack was expected on

our line at daylight, to relieve that place if possible, and that, therefore, head-quarters would probably move. So it turned out; at six we heard that the French had all crossed the Bidassoa, and were moving on. The baggage was all ordered half a league up the mountain Yangi, there to wait orders either to proceed further for security if we were pressed, or to return if we repulsed the attack. At seven, Lord Wellington, &c., were off. By nine the town was nearly cleared, and every one in motion.

Nothing can be more stupid than thus waiting a whole day standing with the mules and baggage, to hear the result, without a creature to talk to, and knowing nothing that is passing. One of the officers advised me to go up the hill just above Lezaca, to observe a little what was doing near, assuring me that it was quite safe. Just afterwards Major Canning returned from Lord Wellington with orders, and said he would show us the way to the hill and then go on. I mounted, and set out with Henry, having sent off my baggage. Mr. Booth, the principal Commissary of Accounts, Mr. Jesse, his assistant, and Captain Hook, the officer who takes all the quarters for every one at head-quarters, determined to join the party. When we had got a little way Major Canning remarked that by

going up the first hill we should see sooner what
was doing, and could then return to Lezaca, or
stay and proceed as was found advisable, and that
we should be thus sure of not being cut off from
Yangi. We did this. When half up the hill
we observed two battalions resting under arms
quietly on the top, and having examined them
some time with our glasses, thought them Spanish ;
but not being certain, (as they are so alike as
scarcely to be known at fifty yards distance,) we
thought it advisable to keep to our left, towards
the rear of some of our own red coats, whom we
saw engaged with the French in a wood further
on. We did this, and then waited to see whether
those two battalions advanced and fired or not, to
enable us to be sure, by their fire, to which party
they belonged. As they remained at rest, we could
not determine this point ; and as there was much
fern and wood, and we were only about a short half
mile off, we determined, for fear of a surprise, to go
back, and follow up the mountain Major Canning's
road, where we saw our own red coats. We did this,
and just before we ascended, ascertained that our
people were still there ; we trusted firmly to their
not giving ground, as the French were already
much advanced, and this road was the common
communication of all our army through Lezaca to
Oyarsun and San Sebastian.

About half way up the hill, or mountain, is a wood, from whence we got a peep of the two battalions. We saw them moving towards the English position, but not firing, and Captain Hook remarked that there were several red coats amongst them, so they must be friends; but that, however, about a hundred yards further on we should be able to ascertain, and if it was not so we must return.

At the end of the hundred yards the wood ceased, and the two roads up the mountain joined, when to our great astonishment, just as we came one way to the place of junction, two French battalions came up the other, and we found ourselves within twenty yards of each other; Mr. Jesse was still nearer. I heard a cry of *qui vive*, which put an end to all doubt as to who they were; and after a sort of short pause and drawback in the head of the French column, thinking, I believe, that they were the head of an allied column, several moved towards us, and two levelled at us. Mr. Jesse, the nearest of us, dismounted, and surrendered instantly. The other two jumped off their horses, and as the side of the mountain was very steep, and no one could well ride after them, they ran down, and the French having incumbrances, I believe, they escaped. I now think that was the best plan I could have adopted. At the moment, however, as I was in the road, and nearer to the

French than they were, I determined to turn about, and try my horse down the road again, the way we came, thinking it a great chance that the only two who levelled, and seemed ready to fire, would hit me. They never fired, but some pursued, and one or two officers on horseback. I gallopped down, however, nearly a mile, at the risk of my neck. The road then got steeper, and I looked round to see if any one was nearly up behind me. I pulled up a little, as I found they had not reached my servant, who was above a hundred yards behind me; but, on turning round again to proceed, I saw, in the narrow part of the road just before me, where the descent was steep both ways, one up and one down, six Frenchmen; two in the road, two on each side, all ready with their pieces up to their shoulder. Upon this, I pulled up, and we had a parley. On my pulling up, and addressing them in French, they seemed in doubt, and spoke some bad French. I then looked about me, to see what chance remained, but seeing that they all levelled again, and cried out—"*Prisonnier !*" the risk was then too great for the remotest chance of escape, so I dismounted, and they instantly took down their pieces, and ran up. In a moment, my two horses, and cloak, pistols, sword, telescope, handkerchief, were all gone.

Having received some money just before, and fearing some theft from my Portuguese servants, I had about fifteen doubloons about me, as being the most secure place. One half they found instantly, and were so pleased, that they scarcely searched more, except to take my knife, comb, &c. I then told them that I was no General, having heard a cry before from the battalion of "*Voilà le Général!*" that I was only a civil officer, a non-combatant; but that I had some more money, and if they would then, when they had got everything from me, release me, I would tell them where it was, and give it to them. This I did, thinking as they had got so much booty, they would perhaps wish to keep it secret, not to be called upon to refund any part, and that therefore they would not be sorry to say that I had escaped, and let me go that I might not have to tell the story.

They promised this, so I produced the rest, and at the same time contrived to give my watch a twist up above my waistcoat, that when they felt for it, they found nothing, and by this means I contrived to save it.

The other speculation did not answer so well, as I believe they still took me for a General. They would not release me, and I was carried into the battalion, and then to General D'Armagnac (I

believe), who was behind their attacking troops.
They were leading me into the fire of our own
people, when an officer ordered them up on one
side. I said it would be very hard to get me
killed by our own fire, and that they had better
let me run across, and shoot at me themselves.
Upon the whole they all behaved very civilly, and
without any violence. I there met Mr. Jesse. I
told our story to General D'Armagnac. He said
we were very unlucky, and seemed good-humoured,
ordering the captors to give me back two doubloons. After telling his aide-de-camp to take
us to General Clausel, who commanded in chief
there, and then to the rear, he said he would
apply to get us exchanged (as that was now the
fashion, and not to release civilians gratis) for two
civil officers, friends of his, in England; and then,
lending me one of his horses to ride back upon,
took leave of us. The soldiers told me he had
bought my horse for a trifle, and thus ended the
fate of poor Blackey!

The whole was the work of half an hour. Whilst
we were in the wood, our people had just given
way across this road to superior numbers, and had
thus left us exposed to this misfortune in a place
where every one had passed in safety all the
morning, and so again from an hour later all the

evening. A little sooner, or a little later, we should
not have been caught above a league within our
lines of the morning. Such, however, was our fate!

We were then taken to General Clausel, and
were instantly ordered back to his former head-
quarters. There was then a great out-cry for
ammunition, which delayed the French some time,
and, as they said, saved our last position on this
hill. I found that they did not, however, know
the country well, and tried to pump me as to what
was beyond, both as to men, and mountains, &c.
I always pleaded ignorance as a civilian. They
had contrived to get four small two-pounder field
mountain-pieces up this difficult ascent, and kept
them constantly in use, asking me why we, who
were so ingenious, did not adopt the same practice? I said they had taught us the art of war,
and I believe they had found their scholars had
made very rapid progress, so that if these guns
were really worth the labour, I had no doubt we
should soon have some, but that such things were
not to be found ready-made in the mountains,
therefore they must wait a little. I soon gave up
my horse to a wounded man, as they abounded on
the road, and we descended and crossed the Bidassoa by the ford below the bridge, as I found our
light division were still maintaining their ground

near the bridge at Bera (or Vera), and had kept
the other side of the valley all the time secure.

A tremendous storm then began. We took
shelter till five o'clock in a hovel, but at last proceeded, the storm continuing, up the mountain of
La Rune, to the French position, and head-quarters,
—those of General Clausel. Mons. d'Arnot, an
officer belonging to the latter, was extremely kind
to us. He said our best prospects were not to stay
and sleep in the hovel, where we should be starved
and crowded by wounded, &c., but to go with him
to the General's hut on the top, where if anything
was to be had, we should have it. He also lent
me a horse part of the way up again. We passed
the French position to the entrenched camp, where
amongst a variety of huts of boughs, earth, &c.,
were three rather better than the rest, consisting of a few feather-edged boards at top, and
earth and fern on the sides and bottom. These
were Generals Clausel, Taupin, and D'Armagnac,
for the attendants, &c. There were only two
places where it had not rained in considerably, and
we were wet through, without a change.

The General's canteens were unpacked, and the
aide-de camp said, " If he returns, you will have
some dinner, if not, we have some bread." That
and sour wine was all our fare for the night, and

we laid down in our wet clothes on the ground. They first gave us up General Clausel's dry inner chamber, but on a notice coming that he was returning, we were removed to the attendants' hut. There I passed a sleepless night, our party being the two aides-de-camp, a colonel, a major, five of the gens-d'armes, or police corps, Henry, the General's cook, a friend, two or three attendants, and about four wounded men who staggered in, and lay in the middle. The horses were all tied to the boards out in the storm all night, and making a noise against our heads. The wounded were groaning; then came an oath from an officer against them as cowards, and asking how that noise made them any better? At last came a poor creature with a violent colic; this last filled us as close as we could lie, and constant quarrels ensued between those near the doors or those who came every minute for shelter from the storm and rain, and to get help for their wounds. The lightning gave us a glimpse of the scene every five minutes. Now and then an observation escaped as to the rain swelling the Bidassoa, &c.

At three o'clock the firing began again close to us; at four the drum beat to arms, and at six we got a little cold meat and bread and wine, after the General's breakfast, and about seven we were marched towards St. Jean de Luz with a party of prisoners and deserters. Amongst them were several of the Chasseurs Britanniques, who, with their red jackets, had by deserting to the enemy, and then advancing with them, contrbuted to our being surprised and taken. We stopped half an hour in the wood below, and got a little brandy from the post of the gens-d'armes in the rear, and got to St. Jean de Luz about one o'clock,—three leagues. This was Marshal Soult's head-quarters. Thither we went, and merely saw him in a crowd. We were then taken to Count Gazan, and then to the Commandant of the police, &c. We were quartered at an inn with some gens-d'armes in the outer room; got some supper at seven at General Gazan's, to whom I mentioned what had passed at Vittoria, was allowed to write to head-quarters to let them know where we were, and to ask for money, clothes, &c., if we were not exchanged, and we were allowed to stay till next day to wait for an answer.

No answer came. It was intended to give us horses to carry us to Bayonne the next evening, but all were engaged in carrying away wounded men, including some troops of cavalry, so we marched on foot about three o'clock, five under a guard. We were delayed by the bad walking of some deserters, and were then again caught the last half league in another most furious thunder-storm, which soaked us through in five minutes. At nine we reached this place, three long leagues, and were taken to the Nouveau Fort. The Marechal de Logis gave us a bed between us, on the ground, in a room with two midshipmen and a sick and wounded officer of the 34th, and having got some bread and cheese, we went to bed, with a dry shirt which he lent us. I have ever since had rheumatism, and am far from well, having considerable pain, at night in particular, and a little fever, but I am now rather better. We occupy a round tower here, and our soldier-prisoners are in the court below; the Spaniards are above, and some sailors in confinement, as their dress would enable them to escape. Our two midshipmen were exchanged the next day. From Mr. Babou, the banker, a most liberal and generous man, we have got money, and therefore now go on well. How officers manage who have no money I cannot guess. Only three of the number the banker has given money to have had their bills protested, and he says if it is poverty he shall never complain, otherwise he should wish to be paid. If I get back I have undertaken to speak to Lord Wellington on the subject.

13th September, Mont de Marsan.—On the 8th

I received a most kind letter from Lord Wellington, in his own handwriting, as to an old friend,
telling me that he authorised me to tell the Duke
of Dalmatia he would send back for me any one
named by him, to be given in exchange.*   I had
just before received a notice to set out next day for
Verdun.   I went with a gens-d'armes instantly to
the General of Division, Baron d'Huillers, and to
the Commandant General Sol.   To them I told my
story, and showed my letter.   They advised me to
send my letter to the Duke of Dalmatia, and engaged to detain me until the answer came back.   I
also asked to write to the duke myself.   The other
officers, who had already been to Moulins (where
General Paget is), wrote also for leave to go to a
nearer depôt than Verdun, on account of the expense they had been put to ; they were of the 34th
regiment, and they also were allowed to wait the
answer.   The other five officers of the 60th were
despatched with a *feuille de route* for Verdun.
On the 9th, about seven o'clock, I went to the
play with two Dutch officers of the 130th
regiment, one of whom was with me when at
La Rune in the camp, and had been all along very
civil, and had called upon us and volunteered going

* See Appendix, at the end.

with us to the theatre. I did this in order to pass
the anxious time away till my answer came. The
play I did not much enjoy, as you may suppose,
though our two gens-d'armes were very well behaved, and went into a box opposite, leaving us
with the officers.

At nine o'clock came an account that my letter
was arrived. I ran home and eagerly opened it
I found it was a very civil answer from Count
Gazan, full of good wishes, &c., but stating Marshal
Soult had never had any proposal made to him for
my exchange by our General, or that it would be
done instantly ; again assuring me that if any such
should arrive I should be instantly sent back, and
that in the mean time orders should be given
that none of us should for the present cross the
Garonne.

The next morning (the 10th) came an order to
be at Mont de Marsan in four days, about seventy
miles off, the chief town of the department of
Landes, and there to wait orders. We also got a
letter to give to the Commandant there to halt the
others there, or to bring them back if they had
passed that depôt I prepared a letter to Lord
Wellington, encouraged by his letter to me (I had
before only written to the Adjutant-general), and
stated to him how matters stood, &c., thanking

him as I felt for his kindness. This I enclosed in one to Count Gazan, in French, and begged him, as a last favour, to forward it by a flag of truce through the lines to Lord Wellington. I then hastily bought a few necessaries, and engaged with the other five officers to be conveyed to this place (Mont de Marsan) in a large coach with six mules, Henry in the driver's tilt-cart in front. When I went home to pay our gens-d'arme, he was most unreasonable and broke his agreement; we would not pay him, so he locked us in. I said I had the General's orders to march at one o'clock, and called upon him at his peril to release us, and to go with us to settle the matter. He would not, but released us, and would then take nothing. I then went off to General Sol, and told my story. He sent for the man in a hurry, but as he did not come instantly, asked what we proposed to give. I told him. He said if we were willing to pay that sum (which was according to our agreement) " Very well, leave it here, and you may set out ; had you left it to me I should not have made you pay nearly so much." Accordingly at two o'clock we started, and got, in four hours and a half, over four leagues of the country, or sixteen miles, to a small village on the river side, where we dined and slept. Our route was

through Dax and   , but we had leave,
as that was knee-deep in sand, to pass by Orthez.

Next morning (the 11th) at four o'clock, we
proceeded to Orthez to breakfast, and got there, six
leagues, by eleven o'clock.   There we sat down to
a *dejeuné à la fourchette*, that is, a regular dinner
in every respect, but not so comfortable as at our
little village the night before.   We then at one
started again, and before six got to Hugemont,
where we dined again, and slept four leagues
further.

On the 12th, at seven, we set out for this place,
through the heavy sand in some places, and
over a ruinous bridge ; we did not arrive until
twelve.   We found everything all along the road
in a state of the greatest activity for the supplies of
the army, everything in requisition.   I longed to
have some of the Spaniards with me, to teach them
what was to be done in this way.   The love of
coffee is much diminished, and the lower classes
are excluded from it by the high price of that and
of sugar.   Other things are cheap, and we got our
dinner, beds, and all for five francs a-head each
night.   Our mules were very fine, and each had
a name, which we soon learnt, by the constant
dialogues of the old driver and his boy, one of the

two latter always running by the mule's side, as there were no reins to the other four in front.

We met with every attention and civility here, were in time to stop our other five officers, and we are now all in officers' billets, the same as the French officers themselves, and have received for our days of march the same as they do on the march,—a captain three francs, a colonel five, a lieutenant two and a half, &c. I am at the house of the principal engineer (from Paris) of some works going on here, Monsieur De Beaudre. Great improvements are nearly completed in this little departmental capital : a new wide stone bridge of easy access, instead of an old narrow gothic one, and an open space cleared around it ; a new Prefect's palace, with departmental offices, &c. A new chapel, new official houses, and much private repairs, are in progress : this is very unlike Spain. I breakfast alone in my billet on my tea, which I have discovered here, as the others have only meat and wine. I dine with the rest,—and to please them, but against my will,—at six ; we have a good cheap dinner at four francs each. The poor officers do not know what to do with themselves. I immediately applied to my patron for books, and he gave me the range of several. After a play or two of

Racine's, and a few of the *Contes Moraux*, I have attacked La Harpe's *Cours de Littérature* at the Lycée, and am as yet well pleased ; I walk as much as·my rheumatism permits. Thus goes time ; but I suffer much,—I feel as if I had been broken on the wheel.

Poor Henry is more bewildered than ever, but flatters himself he shall soon learn French. If he could copy the activity around him, he would be wonderfully improved. We are here full of the *Moniteur's* victories, and the little check the French appear to have sustained latterly under Vandamme in Bohemia.

Before I go to bed I get my cup of coffee, a small one indeed, for my ten sous, at the café, read the news and then retire home. This place is very full, from the wounded being in part here ; from the exertions making as to supplies, as we have two hundred cars here in a day ; from some artillery drivers being here, and from the constant passage of everything to and from the army. The Commandant has been particularly obliging. We have a mile round the town to walk in, and are never troubled by any one.

Oyarjan, in Spain, at the Head-Quarters of General Graham, October 4th, 1813.—Once more

again at liberty, as far as my rheumatic limbs will
permit: the will, at least, is free, and I hope soon
my arms and legs will be so likewise.

On the 21st, at Mont de Marsan, arrived my mules,
pony, and baggage; no letter. I gave up all prospect of exchange, and was stupidly ill and tranquil.
The lady where I was quartered was very attentive
and good-natured, and I had begun my literary
course, and had made up my mind to my fate. On
the 22nd, however, at nine, came an order for us all
to set out at eleven for Bayonne again. We did
so, had some little misfortunes, overturns, &c., but
got to the Chateau Vieux at Bayonne, on the
25th September, and had the honour of being confined in the same room where Palafox had been for
three months, and all the great Spanish prisoners,—
the Duke of Gravina, Prince of Castel Franco, &c.
We staid there, seven of us, until the 1st, in
anxious suspense,—the room too noisy for reading,
and I too ill for it, so we played whist, and killed
time in that way quietly. At five o'clock on the 1st,
when at dinner, came an order for Mr. Jesse and
myself only to set out at six for St. Jean de Luz, in
the dark. We got a coach at six, the only vehicle
to be had, and I packed all my baggage, and
mounting Henry and my Portuguese on the mules
we arrived all at eleven at night at the Police at

St. Jean de Luz. We were sent to an inn for the night, then the next morning (the 2nd) taken to Count de Gazan, at ten. I found him very civil, had much conversation with him for an hour, breakfasted with him, and at twelve we were all packed off with an escort for Endaye, to be sent over here.

The gens-d'armes took us first to Count Reille, whose quarters were half a league on from St. Jean de Luz. He sent us on to General Maucale, who was half a league further. He gave us a fresh escort, and sent us round the end of the lines, down to the water side at Endaye. All very civil in every way. At Endaye, about four, we were with some danger sent across, mules and all, in a little flat-bottomed boat to Fontarabia to the Spanish outpost. There also much civility, but much delay. At five we got to Irun with a Spanish escort, were taken to General Frere, found him at dinner,— very civil, but gave us nothing to eat. I then went to General Stopford; he was at dinner. No quarters to be had, so I sent my baggage on here, but got some dinner. At eight, came on in the rain here; found General Graham; very kind. He gave me a bed in his quarters, and some tea. Breakfasted here this morning; baggage gone to Lezaca; I go there in half an hour. I am grown very thin, and am in very crazy condition, but must get patched up at head-quarters, and go to work again. This last month has been like a dream. I hear there has been much difficulty about my exchange; but it is now over, I am happy to say, and Lord Wellington has been very kind. I hope to do something for my fellow prisoners when I see him.

Count Gazan has asked me to get for him the following print or caricature to complete a collection he has. Will you do your best to find it, and send it out if possible. The Count's description:—

" Une caricature qui a paru a il y a douze ou quinze ans à Londres, au sujet d'un voyage que fit dans cette capitale Le Grand Rabbin Juif d'Hollande, dans l'intention de reformer la manière de vivre des Juifs de Londres dans ce temps là."

[N.B.—It was not possible to trace or find this print, though every inquiry was made.]

Lezaca, Head-Quarters, October 7th, 1813.— To day I have a little leisure, as every one is engaged out, and a grand attack is to be made on the French position to drive them quite off that mountain, La Rune, where I got my rheumatism. It will be, I fear, tough work; I dare not go and peep again, even if I were well enough, so have taken up this paper. Baggage and all for the present remain here, only ready to load in case of necessity.

Lord Wellington had much difficulty in procuring my exchange, and has been very kind; indeed, every one here has appeared very much interested in my return, and "my French value." The Commissary-at-War was treated here like a prince, to procure me every favour, when he went back, by his representations. In short, if my pain goes off, I shall not regret my other losses, which amount to about 230*l*., but shall feel myself a very fortunate man upon the whole.

Monsieur Babedac, the banker at Bayonne, is most liberal and kind to all the English officers taken. I hear a hundred have had money from him; only five bills of 110*l*. in the whole have been sent back unpaid; this, I hope, Lord Wellington will pay, though the banker said, if distress occasioned it, he did not wish it. Nearly all my baggage is now collected safely through the kindness of friends. I have been, as you may suppose, much questioned by Lord Wellington, &c., and many now seem to envy me the trip, as it has ended so well.

I will now fill up my former French letter a little more freely. On the morning following, the scene at the French head-quarters at St. Jean de Luz was very curious. First, came rumbling back from the attack seven brigades, or about forty-two pieces of ordnance, with the ammunition-waggons about a hundred, looking very gloomy, almost all drawn by mules, and generally in good condition. You will here observe how soon the French come about again. Then came the pontoon bridge, and, lastly, perpetual strings of cars, with the wounded. The poor country people shaking their heads and lamenting all this misery, all wishing for peace, and all saying it was their Emperor who prevented it, from his unbounded ambition. This was the talk of the officers, and of all. They said the Allies, if successful, would rise in their demands; that Bonaparte was too proud to yield, and peace would only be farther off than ever. This was the conversation, when they heard of the check in the North.

When the account of the first victory of the 25th came (which, by-the-bye, was the first information received as to the quarrel with Austria), they were all in high spirits, and exclaimed—"Ah! le pauvre beau Père, il sera chassé," and "Peace from the North will either give us peace here also, or enable us to drive you all back to Portugal with the reinforcements which we shall obtain." Things changed afterwards, and three weeks after the bulletin of the 25th, &c., and only the day before the bad bulletin came out, a Te Deum had been ordered at Bayonne, and an hundred *coups de canon* for the first victory! The people almost laughed at this themselves, though very miserable.

At the inn at St. Jean de Luz, where I was billeted with a gens-d'armes at the door, we were allowed to dine with the officers, who were all returning starved from the lines to get a belly-full. I here met with men of a superior description, Colonels of the Guards, Chief Medical Officers, Post-Masters, Commissaries, &c. They were civil, some of them gentleman-like and free in their conversation, much irritated at having been beaten by the Spaniards, which, with a tirade about numbers, they admitted to be the fact. Monsieur D'Arnot, a young man attached to General Clausel, and a young Dutch officer, gay, tall, and handsome, were the most attentive to us, and without any object, which most of the others had in view, to get a wife back, or a lost portmanteau, their letters, &c.

The people all told us that had we been quite prepared to advance into France at first, Bayonne was open, and without guns, dismantled; that we might have walked in and gone on to Bordeaux. I believe much of this, but not entirely, and our men were nearly as much harassed as the French. The French troops in the first confusion behaved very ill, and plundered the inhabitants, throwing away their arms, and absolutely flying.

Marshal Soult's orders on this subject were stronger even than Lord Wellington's were here. The inhabitants generally said they would remain quiet if the English came alone, and would leave the armies to settle it, for all they wanted was peace; but that as they knew how the Portuguese and Spaniards had been treated, and what they might therefore expect in return, they must all fly if the allies came with us.

Count Gazan is elderly, and I believe quite sick of his trade; he said he wanted peace and to go to his villa at Nice for life after twenty years' war. He gave me an invitation there. In general all the officers and men were attentive and civil; some looked sulky, but most noticed us by touching the cap, which is more than we do by them here. In a dispute which Captain S—— had with a stupid old fool, the *Commandant de la Place* at Bayonne, General Sol, the French officers present seeing the General was in the wrong (as he afterwards admitted), all bowed to Captain S——, and the General's own sentinel carried arms to him as he went out. This is flattering. The curiosity is very great about Lord Wellington, as one of the great men of the age.

From the questions put to me when taken, about the grand position—and on the way to St.

Sebastian, I am sure the French had a very imperfect notion of the exact state of that part of the mountains. My being a civilian was my excuse for giving them no information. Their loss in getting back again would have been greatly increased, had they got on to the next hill. As it was, from the river swelling, and the men not being able to cross the ford at which I passed, but being obliged to go round by Vera bridge, which was under our fire, their loss was very severe. Had I not been put across early I should have had that fire to pass through with them.

The country all the way to Bordeaux is barren and unproductive; mostly sandy heath with vines, and a few meadows near the stream. I saw no corn, only the Indian corn, and that much less luxuriant than here, and with very little head of green for forage. The consequence is, the French provisions and forage come from an immense distance, and the supplies are very difficult to procure; the exertions, however, are in proportion, and very unlike those in Spain of the Spaniards. Everything for two hundred miles and more round is in requisition, all the corn taken, and only *bons* given in return; wine the same; hay the same—every merchant's car in the town, and all the country cars with oxen at work for the public. The districts off the roads send in to the depôts on the high roads; from thence the corn, &c., is forwarded to the army, to the depôts at Bayonne, &c. The hay comes for the staff horses and cavalry, as Gazan told me himself, one hundred leagues, that is, nearly three or four hundred miles, from above Toulouse, &c., partly by water, but much by land. The people now feel for the first time what it is to supply their own army in their own country, and the grievance is no small one.

The army have had a half month's pay; twenty months are due. The prospect of payment of the *bons* for the supplies is very remote indeed; and yet though they all grumble, they act with zeal and spirit; and I still think, with the feelings of Frenchmen, would all unite against invasion. In spite of all this, things in general are still comparatively cheap; dear to Frenchmen, as they say exorbitant—to us reasonable, except colonial produce: bread about 4 sous a pound, or 2*d*. English; and good meat about 8*d*. English, retailed; vegetables and fruit very cheap; wine the same; oats and hay tolerably so, even as I fed my animals, three, at the inns for the day for about 12 or 14 livres travelling, three feeds of corn— small ones, to each about 6 livres, or, as I generally gave them, 8 livres. Hay about 6 or 7 livres, and good— cheaper when

I bought the articles at Mont de Marsan. A good dinner at the inns, with a bottle of light wine, about 5s. each. This sometimes also covered the beds where we slept. Tea only to be had by ounces at a time as medicine ; coffee, very dear ; sugar (brown), from 4s. 6d. to 6s.; white sugar, 7s. the pound.

The consequence has been, in a great measure, to put an end to the great use of coffee: it is now a luxury for the rich, and even they generally breakfast à *la fourchette*, and drink little of it. Of *Syrup de raisin*, I bought a basin-full for about 9d. This is a sort of vinous treacle, and gives a taste to tea as if it were taken from a dirty wine-glass. The *bête rave* sugar was to be had some-times at Bayonne, but I did not meet with any. On some bad sugar being brought to him one day, a French Lieutenant-colonel, by way of abuse, called it *bête rave*, and said, it was only from some small sticks being in it, as really he had seen *bête rave* sugar as good as any other : they still, however, give 6s. a pound for brown island sugar.

The Chateau-Neuf, at Bayonne, was just like an English sponging-house. With money we were very well off. The man, however, cheated us ; we quarrelled; I got redress from the General ; and on my return got into the Chateau-Vieux instead, an old English castle, where we were in the same room as I told you where Palafox, &c., had been ; the Commandant, a gentleman-like man —his wife a troublesome skin-flint. The Commandant at Mont de Marsan was uncommonly liberal to us all ; so were the people there ; equally so, my patron and patrona ; the civil engineer, Baron d'Huilliers, who first commanded at Bayonne, was also civil, but more distant. He is now gone to Bordeaux, and General Thevenot, the late Commandant at Vittoria, has succeeded him. Their reports were, that Soult was going to the north to replace Berthier, who was sick, and Suchet was to succeed in command here. Count Gazan, however, did not admit this, but never positively denied it. It was also said, that the Etat Major would remove to Bordeaux for the winter-quarters. Perhaps the events of to-day may hasten this. The firing is brisk all this time. We met three cavalry regiments on the retreat towards Pau and Toulouse for forage ; the horses in fair order, but generally very inferior to ours in size, &c. ; the men very fine, which was so much the worse for the animals who had to carry them. At one place, near Lain, the depôt of forage was empty. I met a man running hard with orders, the Major's messenger ; he was charged to inform the few neighbouring parishes, that unless they furnished and provided ready at the depôt so many rations of forage for three days for two squadrons of cavalry about to pass by twelve next day, all fit to move on immediately, the squadrons would be halted there that day to help themselves in the vicinity.

Small horses and mules were very cheap, as the forage rations were stopped to the subaltern officers in France, and they all consequently wanted to sell, and many of the country people from the requisition wanted also to sell. Bayonne was declared in a state of siege for the purposes of police. One order of the police posted up in the café Wagram at Bayonne directed, that no politics were to be discussed under pain of arrest. Out of the town, in the suburbs of St. Esprit, was a magnificent hotel, quite in the English style: there our party stopped, but were marched off to the chateau. The activity exhibited by the French Commandant about Bayonne has been very great; one hundred and twenty guns have now been mounted, of one sort or another, instead of about three. This number has been collected all round the country, and new works are rising round the place every day. The young conscripts of the usual levy were being drilled; they were fine young lads of about seventeen or eighteen; too young for Spain, but who in a short time would make excellent soldiers ; at first they appeared dull and a little unhappy ; but in a few days they became gay like the rest.

The newly-raised thirty thousand for the twenty-four departments for Spain were not yet out, but are to be out this week. I understood they will be better men, being taken from the old lists of those who had previously escaped, some of them twenty-five years old. This grievance is very great, but the conscripts seem to forget it themselves, and the old parents can do nothing. It will tell, however, some time or other, I think ; and I hope soon. My patrona told me that her sister's husband had been drawn five years since, got off on payment of two thousand francs, and two francs per day since ; he is now married, has two children, and is still liable to be called upon again. A wish for peace follows the relation of all these stories.

On the whole I was well treated, and I should say that in general the treatment of prisoners by the French is very good. Officers are allowed fifty francs a month to live upon, and on marching, the same *indemnité* as the French ; 5s. a Colonel and Major, 3s. a Captain, and 2s. 6d. a subaltern. Our being able to obtain money makes all the difference almost between our treatment and that of the

Spanish officers, whom they dare not trust on their parole, so many having broken it. The worst treatment I experienced was being marched on foot from St. Jean de Luz to Bayonne, after having been promised a horse, with our own deserters, and kept back until we were caught in a thunder-storm, because these fellows could not or would not march. The soldiers are like themselves to the last ; when marched as prisoners, they jumped over the fences to get apples. The French guard stared, but permitted it to be done.

October 7th, three o'clock.—The passing officers from the front tell me that all is going on well—that the French have given way almost everywhere, though they still hang to the high rocks on La Rune, near where I slept on the 31st. They say the Spaniards have behaved well, but that the 52nd and second battalion of the 95th have suffered, while forcing the position through which I was marched in that thunder-storm. We have no orders to move here at present. The reports confirm the news that I brought in to Lord Wellington, that Soult has gone, and that Suchet commands. I know nothing accurately now, however, as I must not go and peep again for myself.

To return to France, and my dream there—for such it has appeared—I must give you a notion of

a French placeman in a little way, not like our
great sinecurists. My running friend, who carried
the message about the forage, accompanied me side
by side for a league. The people wished him joy
of his prosperity—I asked him why? He said,
" They think that I am making a fortune, having
a place in the hospital; and what do you suppose
it is? I am the hospital sexton; I bury all the
dead, four or five in the twenty-four hours, and all
at night, digging half the night. And for what?—
for eighteen sous (or ninepence English) a-day.
This is not the way to make a fortune you will
allow. My companion makes a better thing of it:
he is always tipsy, and leaves me to dig, but he
always sings as he goes to the grave. The people
who know his voice say, ' There goes poor silly
John,' and give him a sous."

Now for a trait of a gens-d'armes—a private in
the ranks. We went to the play at Bayonne with
a gens-d'armes and our friend, the Dutch officer.
On going down to the coffee-room, my companion,
Mr. Jesse, meaning to be generous, but not understanding the method of treating a revolutionary
gens-d'armes, told him to get anything he wished
to drink as we did. Upon which he flew into a
rage, said he had drank with his Colonels, Majors,
Captains, and had never been sent out to drink like

a servant before. Our Dutchman was obliged to explain to him, in order to pacify him, the difference in our service between officers and privates; said it was once so in France and in Holland, but that the prejudice was removed there now, though it remained in England. He then desired him to sit down and drink with us. With difficulty he was persuaded, and we all knocked our glasses together, and it ended amicably. I did not expect this. The military equality, however, is the only remnant of the Revolution.

The two midshipmen in prison with us amused us much. By mistake, they were at first put in prison with their men for two days on bread and water. They were afterwards in the same room in which I was. We were five in all at first. They slept in the same bed, and were as often alternately with their heads where the feet of the others were as on the pillow. In their open letter to Sir G. Collier, about their exchange, sent in through the French, they suggested the advisability of bringing in two gun-boats close to St. Jean de Luz, in order to prevent' communication with St. Sebastian, and further, advised a little bombardment, &c. The men, as they were marched, proposed to the midshipmen to upset the heavy gens-d'armes by their great jack-boots; said they would never be able to right themselves again, and that they, the sailors, might get off. The officers told them it would not do ; so they were quiet.

October 8th, 1813, *Lezaca.*—The result of yesterday's operations was, that the French were driven from all the mountainous parts of their position above Endaye, opposite Fontarabia, and so along, opposite Irun, to above Bera. I do not know that we have lost above five hundred men in this part. The French did not fight well, and were not above twelve or fourteen thousand here. What has passed higher up I know not. It is said that the sixth division, near Maya, have lost men. I believe Lord Wellington very prudently stopped short, in this part, near Orogne, on the road to St. Jean de Luz, not knowing exactly the result near Maya and Roncesvalles.

It is thought that the French must be in greater strength there, since they are so weak here. Report says, however, that men have been sent northwards. Our sixty pieces of artillery were all carried across the Bidassoa last night, and are established on the main road. We have not lost many officers. About three hundred prisoners were brought in here, with eight officers, about ten o'clock this morning. How lucky that my exchange took place before this, or it would have been at least deferred, or I should have been sent back to the rear.

General Graham has just called on me. He is on his way to England to-morrow; he had called to see Lord Wellington. General Graham was very civil, and assures me that my new mare is a good purchase; and so it ought to be for four hundred dollars. Major Stanhope sold her some time since for a hundred guineas, to take it back at the same if he returned. He did so. General Cole gave him a hundred guineas when he was ordered away again; this looks well.

Evening.—The French still cling with three companies to a rock in the midst of La Rune mountain, about half a mile from my resting-place, now six weeks ago. The Spaniards cannot drive them out. Little has been attempted or done to-day.

The day before yesterday, a curious scene occurred at General Pakenham's. A French militia Captain had been taken among the rocks—a *ci-devant* regular officer retired, and now apparently an active, useful man, in organizing the Basque peasantry. He had some regulars with him, and peasants without uniform. Lord Wellington had succeeded in frightening him by threatening to hang him for invading Spain with peasants. He

seemed a country mountain squire, and rather
simple, though probably useful. He let out much
against Bonaparte, and told us many truths. He
was told that I had just come from beyond Bayonne,
and made me confirm it by many facts. He was
surprised and puzzled, but believed I had been
there as a spy, and never guessed the truth.
Another officer, who knew about eight words of
Basque, was passed off as a proficient in Basque.
The poor militia officer stared, but swallowed
everything as easily as his dinner. His own
account of the chase of him by the Portuguese,
the rocks he climbed whilst they fired, given in the
most animated style, was very entertaining. I was
almost sorry this unlucky Basque squire was to
leave us next morning for Passages, to learn a
little English farming. He confessed that if he
had been a single man, and had not left a wife and
servants with six of the 6th Light Regiment board-
ing in his house, he should in these times have been
rather glad than otherwise to have got away to England, to avoid the present troubles. What he wished
for most, however, was to return on parole, as he
could then be at home quietly, with an excuse to
enable him to refuse to take any part in what
was doing. The arming of the country being what

Lord Wellington wished to prevent, he could not, of course, favour this man.

9th October, five o'clock.—The French have given up the rock on La Rune in the night, and have to-day been beaten out of two or three redoubts, but there has been but little else done, and some say we shall now be quiet again until Pamplona falls. To-morrow, head-quarters move to Bera, only half a league. Bera is a large ruined village. A letter has been intercepted from Pamplona, stating that the 25th of this month will be the very latest they can hold out; but we have heard this already very often. It draws nearer the truth, certainly, every time. Plunder has begun, and disorder in the French villages, and Lord Wellington is highly angry. He says, if officers will not obey orders, and take care that those under them do so also, they must go home, for he will not command them here; so many of our officers seem to think they have nothing to do but to fight.

This place, Lezaca, is grown very unwholesome, like an old poultry-yard, and the deaths of the inhabitants are very numerous. So, I think, there is no reason to regret the change. I can never be worse off, for I am half eaten up by fleas.

CHAPTER V.

PICTURESQUE QUARTERS—SPANISH REVERSES—A STRANGE
ADVENTURER—SPANISH JEALOUSY—DISTRIBUTION OF THE
ARMY—A PLEASANT COMPANION — NEWS FROM THE NORTH
—MORALE OF THE FRENCH ARMY—THE ARTILLERY.

Head Quarters, Bera or Vera,
Oct. 15, 1813.

MY DEAR M——,

I HAVE now a quarter with a most rural exterior, and a balcony all along the upper storey, hung with vines. The picturesque and the comfortable, however, are not always combined, for the room is dirty, has a fair share of fleas, and though small, has four windows, with only large wooden shutters, and no fire-place. It will be but a cool winter residence, and I fear even less comfortable in fact than my Frenada habitation. The ground-floor is the stable, the centre devoted to me and to the family, the upper storey a great drying-room. The style is, however, pretty.

Several of the best houses are destroyed, nearly all gutted of furniture, chairs, tables, &c., and many deprived of doors and shutters, for the French camp. Some wounded occupy some of the best houses, and in addition to Lord Wellington's staff, head-quarters, and Marshal Beresford's, who has returned from Lisbon, we have General Cole's staff here, and General Alten's. This place was for two months a sort of neutral ground between the two armies, so you may guess that it is a little deranged. It has been populous, and contained a considerable number of spacious houses, though not magnificent; yet the room Lord Wellington occupies is, upon the whole, better than almost any one he has had since Madrid. It is well proportioned, has clean walls, and is sufficiently capacious to admit twenty-five or thirty persons to dinner well. Of course he furnishes it, as there are only bare walls. The largest house in the place, and the best in point of situation, on a pretty knoll above the town, was made what is called a strong house of, and a regiment of Portuguese are now in it. The squire, I fear, has not gained by this arrangement.

The Spaniards were disturbed early yesterday morning about two miles from this, surprised, and driven from a redoubt, with some loss in prisoners and wounded. I believe, however, they behaved well afterwards ; but a Spanish regiment gave way. That queer playhouse hero, Downie, who was there as a volunteer, rallied them, and conducted them well, but had his horse wounded. He once more exhibited on the Pyrenees the sword of Pizarro, which had so narrow an escape when he was made prisoner in the South. You may remember that he threw it back to his friends across a broken bridge, when he was wounded and cut off by the French. He is, I believe, very brave, and seems to take with the Spaniards, though with us he can scarcely speak without exciting a smile, or even more. He was first a Commissary in the light division.

The day before this little surprise, the English officers at General Cole's were remarking that it was only surprising that the Spaniards kept the redoubt and their post ; for the officers were never seen there with the men to keep them on the alert, and the men were cooking without arms within twenty yards of the French sentries, quite uncon-

cerned. I hope this little surprise may save us
from a greater; but I expect some night that the
French will make a night attack upon the
Spaniards, though that is contrary to their usual
method, which is generally to march two hours before day-light, and begin the attack at break of day.

15th, later.—I have just met Downie, and he
says Lord Wellington has admitted that the French
were too strong for the Spaniards, and that he had
given them a fort to defend too much in advance in
the French position. The result, however, is that
the French have kept the redoubt, and are at work
on it already, and have recovered every house
in the suburbs of Zera, or Sara, of which the
Spaniards at one time had nearly one half. Many
say that this is properly a part of the French position, and does not signify at all. Lord Wellington
seems to have a bad cold to-day.

Every one appears to have had some adventures
the night I was taken prisoner. General Pakenham's
horse and Captain Eckersley's fell down from a
bank into the river below, and it was so dark that
they and two others thought it best to remain there
in the trees till daylight, and not stir though it

rained. Lord Wellington and all his staff lost their way, and were five hours exploring two leagues home in the rain and dark, and did not arrive until ten at night, after various perils. It was a tremendous night. Mr. Heaphy, the artist, who is now here, was nearly being involved in my scrape, and it is said he has, in consequence of these risks, added ten guineas to the price of his likenesses, and made them fifty guineas instead of forty guineas. This is too much for a little water-colour whole length; but he has, I hear, now taken twenty-six, and some excessively like.

Some of our houses begin to improve much, as many of the inhabitants, who must be somewhat used to these events, are returning now with all their doors and shutters, &c., which they had themselves carried off and concealed. Canning's quarter is suddenly by this means transformed into a comfortable sort of residence.

Head Quarters, Vera, October 16.—Here I am, still sticking to my post, though in constant pain, and at times bent enough to act the old woman, like Mrs. Sparkes. The doctor still says I must, first or last, go to the hot-bath at Sestona, but

I fight off as long as I can, and shall remain on unless I get worse. Things must, I think, mend soon. I am satisfied, from the pain in my side and chest, that stomach and bile, or " Mr. Liver," is at the bottom of the whole ; but the provoking thing is, I can get no digestible plain food. The ration beef is like shoe-leather ; mutton I can scarcely ever get; fowls are 9s. each, and are all snapped up before my man can resolve to give that price for them. Pork, ham, sausages, salt-fish and bacon alone abound, and these constantly disagree with me. So much for the day. In the night I am confined to my little portmanteau bed, and can scarcely, after a few hours, turn without ten minutes exertion, in the course of which I generally get a knock against the iron. And then my bedfellows are so abundant that you would scarcely credit how I am tormented and eaten up by their kindness and affection. Nothing but the famous Russian " General Frost," can put an end to these persevering and voracious enemies. I shall try to-day, for dinner, broth, mashed potatoes, and roasted apples only, and in spite of this pain, mean to ride the mare in the meadows for an hour.

Every one seems to think we shall make no other movement until Pamplona falls, which, as usual, is daily expected. The French, in the meantime, are in busy preparation, burrowing and throwing up works like moles, on every rising ground near them. I do not think that they ever really intended to defend this mountain La Rune; they were in some degree surprised, as I told you; they had a notion that we had sent two divisions to Catalonia. They now, I think, will fight harder for each acre of ground, unless completely turned by numbers, and a decided flank movement from Roncesvalles.

From what I hear, and the whole of which I dare not mention, I fear the Spanish Government and Lord Wellington have not gone on well together lately, in spite of outward appearances. The moment any General acts cordially with us, and a measure goes on well, some reason is found for his removal. This ridiculous Spanish jealousy would be bearable if they supported it by exertions of their own, so as to enable us to leave them to themselves; but we are now feeding and clothing their half-starved men in the front, and they are doing very little in the rear to supply those they have, or to increase their numbers. In short, five years' misery has not yet scourged them into reasonable beings, and turned romance heroes into common-sense soldiers and practical politicians. The men, however, seem now to fight well whenever they are well led.

October 17th, Sunday, Post-day.—General Graham has acted wisely in going home just now, his age considered. I told Lord Wellington that the French officers said he (Lord Wellington) ought to die now as he never would have such another year, and fortune would prove fickle. He laughed, but did not seem disposed to acquiesce in this. He is better.

I have just got four bundles of English hay, which are to last me for ten days, about a hundred pounds weight each. The next of my forage must be picked up on the hills, or bought in the market in the shape of baskets of coarse river grass.

Head-Quarters, Vera, October 21st, 1813, Thursday.—The week is already half elapsed, and Sunday, the post-day, draws near, leaving me in the same predicament as last week, that is, with nothing to say. I am like the Spanish country people, who, without waiting to hear a question always begin " *nada, nada, nada,*" or "nothing, nothing, nothing." They generally add to us "*Francese roben*" and "*rompas todas,*" and as the French told me, said to them "*Anglesi rompen*" and "*roben todas,*" but always to every one "*nada, nada.*"

As to health, I am upon the whole looking better, and in many respects I feel so. I have this last week ridden out for half an hour every day before breakfast, and an hour or two before dinner ; and thus exercise myself and my horses in the meadows about here, which are now of course all open, and when it has dried up a little after the rain, make a good riding-school.

The only news here just now is, that Marshal Beresford is to have a separate command of a *corps d'armée,* not to act separately, but to complete our system, which will be, General Hill, right column; General Sir J. Hope, left column, which Graham had ; Marshal Beresford the right centre-column ; and Lord Wellington the left centre. Each consisting of different divisions and bodies of the allies.

The French to-day are collecting upon the rising ground near La Rune, and our people, thinking that this looked like a threat of doing something, are all on the watch, but I hear no firing. This is another anxious moment, as the fall of Pamplona is daily expected, and the garrison threaten to blow it up, which will make some desperate work.

Lieutenant-colonel Elphinstone arrived here some time since with Marshal Beresford, from Lisbon. He is now in quarters within a hundred yards of me, across a little stream; my nearest neighbour indeed, except Colonel Ellicombe, in that direction. He is here without his horses, and without much baggage, or many comforts; he is therefore, like myself, buying. His own horses are only now at Ciudad Rodrigo on the road. He has made up his mind to stay till the war is over.

The French, in addition to a few conscripts, who have joined, have called out all the militia in the neighbouring departments. This is a new scene, but I have still great doubts of the policy of entering France at all. The French now suffer severely, and grumble against their own Government. Invasion may stir up the strong vanity of a Frenchman, and make him forget his grievances, in order to revenge himself on those who insult his native soil. Five or six subaltern officers have come over here to us; I believe from some Spanish connexions generally, or disgust and personal disappointment; and two inhabitants of the village on this side of St. Jean de Luz, Oragne, came over here to avoid serving in the militia, which is now being assembled.

12 *o'clock, Friday, 22nd.*—Nothing was done yesterday. It was all a false alarm in the front. The French, however, say we shall be astonished with some extraordinary news in less than three days! Some say they mean from the North, some from Pamplona. If they are bold enough in the latter to dash out in the night against Don Carlos and his Spaniards, I think they would, with the loss of about one-third of their men, fight their way to Jaca, where they have a garrison, and escape. They would of course come out with only provisions to carry, leave mines prepared to add to the confusion, sally out in all directions, and then push on in a body. Don Carlos with all his vigilance would not be a match for them, I think. He has sent word to the governor that he holds his head

answerable for the safety of the works of the town, and two Frenchmen liable to death for every Spanish inhabitant starved.

Saturday, 23rd.—Rather better, but still broken-backed : and with much business to do. As I have dined alone every day since Sunday last, when I went to Lord Wellington's, I pick up no news. Your July Edinburgh Review is wonderfully fallen off; in parts very tame, and more like a poor imitation of the old Edinburgh Review; and yet some of the articles are curious. We begin to feel the effects of this dangerous coast now. Vessels can even now hardly lie safely, though shut up in the close harbour of Passages; and the last packet was close in on Sunday last, on the same day on which Major Hare fought his way in, in the *Landrail,* and has never been able to land the mail until yesterday. Major Hare brought papers to the 9th, but scarcely any news. He was closely examined by Lord Wellington when he arrived at dinner time. He had got up his lesson so badly, that he could answer nothing clearly as to dates, but always ended by a reference to the papers.

It is known that Bonaparte was at Dresden up

to the 5th instant, and nothing done. This some call bad, some good news. On the whole, I think the latter. Colonel Gordon states that Bonaparte used our position here, as a strong argument with the Emperor of Austria to join him in force, saying nothing could restore matters here but an entire new army of a hundred and fifty thousand men, who had not known the English, and that he should be invaded unless supported by his father-in-law. This is a queer argument to one who, I suspect, was only hesitating through fear of his son-in-law's strength being too much for the Allies, and would tell the wrong way. He also states that, Lord Wellington's true account of Vittoria did harm in Germany, being much under the notions they had entertained of it.

Head-Quarters, Vera, October 24th, 1813.— Post-day, and still nothing to add. We remain *in statu quo.* I see the papers have made rather a pretty history of my capture, treating me as an old gentleman (as just now they well may) and that my younger friends got off. In fact, however, the youngest of the party, Jesse, was the first who was taken. There will soon be some rumpus here among the artillery and engineers on the subject of rank and brevet rank.

Head-Quarters, Bera, or Vera, October 31st, 1813.—I have been so worried this week with business and other things, that I have not been able to write until the very post-day, so this will be, I fear, short and hasty. The weather has been trying, one day very cold, and I hoped we were to have clear frost, which, in spite of my open room, I like better than wet. The thermometer got down to 36°, close to where I was shaving, three mornings since; but it soon turned to wet—raw, constant, violent cold wet; north-west wind and rain in repeated stormy torrents. In camp our poor soldiers have had their tents torn, and almost washed away; then we have had hail, followed by snow. Colonel Belson has written to me very feelingly, from the mountains, but seems well.

Another drawback as to writing has been this :— three brigades of artillery were moved along La Rune mountain, three nights since by night : as they went close to the French pickets, to get from our left to Endage, towards the centre, in our front, they have as yet only reached this vicinity,

and have halted here now. Amongst them was
Colonel Ross's light troops, and Captain Jenkinson,
and young ——; the latter came to me here,
very miserable, wet, &c.; to save him camp, I took
him in. Here he has been three days, and with
my establishment this gives me some trouble. Besides which, one cannot get on well with business,
with a chum always at hand, in a small room, night
and day. He is pretty well, and I conclude will
remain at this place until we move—at least until
the army moves, which every one expects as soon
as the French will give us up Pamplona. This is
en train I conclude. A proposal came out to Don
Carlos some days since, but a most unreasonable
one; namely, to allow them all to go to France, with
arms and baggage, and to be on parole for one year
not to serve against us. This was refused. They
made a great parade of giving our officers white
bread and champagne, and Burgundy, &c., at the
interview. So much for humbug. They said, " See
how *forts* we are." To which we said, " Let us see
how your men are." Every day's delay now is
very provoking. I hope they will soon surrender.

I yesterday mustered up a grand dinner for

——: a shoulder of mutton, hashed beef, eggs and bacon, and pork chops. To day we must have shorter commons : a little fish, some hashed mutton bones, and eggs and bacon ; I hope a little Madeira is still to be had. You will, from this account, say we feast, and some few do, with great pains and trouble. I wish I could get —— another quarter, as I work in general at breakfast, at dinner, in the evening, &c., and a companion is a great inconvenience, though he is very considerate. Pray tell his family, the Colonel, &c., how he is. Captain Jenkinson would not go into a house, but pitched his tent in the wet, and went to bed dinnerless, at four o'clock, from fatigue. He is, however, well now. The work of getting guns along over a clay-road, up a mountain, in the dark, without being allowed to use lights, is no trifling undertaking.

I have just snatched half an hour's ride, but am driven in by rain. My poor pony is quite done up, and only fit for baggage, so I am still on the look-out for another horse.

The news from the North is very good, especially the Bavarian accession ; which, from the papers, I doubted, but which Colonel Gordon says his

brother mentions as fact : Lord Wellington tells
me also, that Government at home believe it to be
correct. The private letters from the Austrian
head-quarters here do not say much in favour of
the Swedish Prince, and seem to think he has much
of French humbug in him—*c'est à voir*. It is also
said that he saves the Swedes, and is always in the
rear, surrounded with guards and twenty sentinels.
They speak well of the Russian troops, and very ill
of the French lads now opposed to them. You will
rejoice to hear that we are to have service here to-
day in the square with some troops. This will not
do for me, standing out bare-headed for an hour in
the damp ; I must remain a heathen a little longer,
I fear. Our lately arrived head-quarters clergyman, Mr. B——, seems to be a pleasant gentleman-like man ; I have, however, only met him
twice.

Two o'clock, Sunday.—Still nothing decisive
from Pamplona. To-day's post brings accounts of
no communication for two days, but that the garrison desert twenty on a day, and say that the place
is almost in a state of mutiny against the General.
To-day the weather has a little cleared up, but our

artillery horses are living upon dried fern and corn
—no hay, no straw, and very little coarse grass:
every one in a fidget to move from hence. Unless
we can so maul this French army, as to have them
at our mercy, and then go where we please, and
stop where we please, out of our own moderation,
I think we shall not have any quiet winter-quarters
this year. As long as anything like an army remains, the French must be doing something to
molest us, unless we molest them; and then the
great nation can never submit to let our allied army
quietly take up their winter quarters in the French
territory—at least I think not. Several of their
conscripts have joined them, and they make a
parade of drilling them within sight and hearing
of our outposts, even in marching without arms,
&c. Their deserters say they have about fifty-five
thousand men; it is supposed with their conscripts
this is rather under the mark. They are throwing
up works in all directions all over the country,
and making breast-works, redoubts, &c. A breast-
work, half round a hill, appears to be turned up in
a few nights.

It must be allowed that they are industrious at
least, but the *morale* of the old soldiers is shaken
very much. It is even said that the young ones
fight the best of the two. This agrees with the

story that we hear from the North : that before
the Austrian ambassador left Paris, a letter from
Marshal Soult had arrived, stating, that unless he
had fifty thousand new men, who had never met
the British, he would not answer for the South of
France.

I see your papers make Endage a fortified place
—it is a great heap of ruins ; never strong, only
once a fortified village. It was nearly destroyed
about the year 1790 by the Spaniards, and has
never recovered itself. In return, Fontarabia, once
really rather a strongly fortified town, was soon
afterwards blown up by the French, and the works
are for the most part still in ruins. The town has
not suffered much, as this was only a military opera-
tion. Of all the ruins we have made amongst us in
Spain, even including Badajoz, and Rodrigo, and
Almeyda, it is said St. Sebastian is the most complete. It was a large, handsome, and thriving
town four months since ; one side of one street
alone remains entire ! every street is barricaded
and blockaded ! Rubbish up to the one pair of
stairs windows, and walls half down, make it dangerous in wind to walk anywhere ; besides which,
the large wooden balconies, hanging about by a few
beams at the two pair of stairs windows, threaten
every moment to fall, even where the walls are

sound. Some repairs are being carried on, however, in a few buildings—at least preparations are
being made by clearing, and the works are in progress towards a state of defence. Most officers think
that the destruction is so great, it can scarcely ever
be a good town again—that is as a town ; as a fortified place with much labour, it may. The French
garrison were so disheartened in the castle, that
they could not be made to do more, as I understand from the engineers, for it was still tenable
some time longer when it surrendered. When the
town was first taken, and our men were all drunk
about the place, committing every disorder, the
Governor was doubting about a sortie to recover it ;
thinking, however, that we must have fresh men
near at hand, in case of such an accident, kept
sober, and together, he gave up the idea. Many
say, that if he had done so, such was the state of
our men, that it would have succeeded. His own
men were very much weakened and dispirited.

Most of the light division tents in front here
have been declared unserviceable from rents, &c.
The men are, as yet, still returned as healthy, to the
astonishment of all, even the doctors, who say the
consequences of this must soon appear. Wine is
dearer, which is a good thing, and I believe our
men bear this cold wet weather better than heat.

Tell John his two newspapers of the 20th have been in great request. I believe only Dr. M'Gregor had one besides Lord Wellington. They have been much read, and I have now enclosed one to Colonel Belson, which will probably be the only one in his division. It happened to contain almost all the news of the last week.

Lieutenant-colonel Elphinstone is still here. I understand that he got a queer answer from Lord Wellington when at Lisbon, which brought him here in such a hurry. When he became senior officer of the corps here, he wrote up for instructions from Lisbon, and to ask what Lord Wellington wished him to do, and where he was to go as Chief Engineer in the Peninsula? The answer was, that as Chief Engineer in the Peninsula, he would best know where his proper place was. Up he came by sea in a week, in consequence.

A man to thrive here must have his wits about him, and not see or feel difficulties, or start them, to go on smoothly. People wonder at Lieutenant-colonel Dickson, Portuguese service, and only (barring brevet rank) a Captain of artillery in our service, commanding as he has done now ever since Frenada, all the artillery of both nations, English and Portuguese. He has four seniors out here, but all young comparatively also, who have submitted hitherto.   E—— says it should be a General's command to be done properly, with proper officers under him; others say the old artillery officers have rather changed their sex, and are somewhat of old women.

Lord Wellington seems rather to favour the latter opinion a little.   I conclude that he finds it answer in practice.   As an instance of this, I may state that in the pursuit after Vittoria in the bad roads, Lord Wellington saw a column of French making a stand, as if to halt for the night.   " Now, Dickson," said he, " if we had but some artillery up !"   " They are close by, my Lord."   And in ten minutes, from a hill on the right, Lieutenant-colonel Rose's light division guns began—Bang—bang—bang !   and away went the French two leagues farther off.   I fear if there had been a General, we should have had, instead of this a report of the bad state of the roads, and the impossibility of moving guns.   In fact, this same brigade of guns, with their mounted men, took the last French mortar near Pamplona, and Lord Wellington passed whilst they were putting it to rights to proceed.   They had killed two of the horses in it the day before.

CHAPTER VI.

FALL OF PAMPLONA—DETERIORATION OF THE ARMY—DUKE
OF YORK'S ORDERS—ORDERS OF MERIT—CHURCH SERVICE
— CAPTURE OF FRENCH REDOUBTS — MARCH OF THE
ARMY—INCIDENTS OF FOREIGN SERVICE—FREQUENCY OF
DESERTION—WELLINGTON AND THE LAWYERS.

Head Quarters, Vera, Nov. 5, 1813.

My dear M——,

HERE we are still, but rather nearer a move
now than when I wrote last. I have never found
a moment to spare to write to you yet this week.
Between business and my chum ——, who is
still here with me, I could never even make a
beginning. Even now, at three o'clock, I have
been five or six hours at work, and must in half an
hour take my ride.

The weather has improved, however, these last
two days, and now tends to frost. This I shall,
in spite of my cold fingers (writing at an open
window), upon the whole benefit by. Anything is

better, I know, than the incessant wet we have
here, all of us, up to that part of the army at Roncesvalles; perpetual torrents from the north-west,
night and day almost, so that the roads have been
nearly impassable. At Roncesvalles they have had
now in the valley fourteen inches deep. So close
as in the valley of Bastan, at Elizondo, it has been
as rainy as here. We have now cold, thick, November, London, foggy mornings, until nearly
eleven o'clock forenoon, and then a clear fine day,
but not yet absolute frost. Thermometer about
36 or 37². Meadows all swampy. On the whole,
however, the snow gentlemen have had much the
best of it, though a little uneasy as to their supplies
just now, from the fear of snow stoppages.

Pamplona has at last fallen, as you will have
learnt last mail, I presume : for, I believe, Lord
Wellington kept the packet on purpose back two
days. The garrison, four thousand two hundred, I
hear, are to embark to day at Passages if possible,
at least, as soon as they can be got ready. Don Carlos
made them submit to his terms, as we hear, *in toto*.
They even were compelled to give up the Juramen-
tudas, besides the fortification artillery. Report
says fifty-seven field-guns have been found there.
This shows us that the danger we escaped by Lord
Wellington's presence of mind, and the bravery of

our fellows on the 28th of July last. Had the
French got a league further, they would have
found this fine field train all ready, and a reinforcement of near five thousand men in the garrison. No one can tell how this might have
changed matters. We have still eighteen guns
here, with the horses living on leaves, fern, and
corn, but ready to play upon a new star-work
the French are every day making more of, on a
hill close to La Rune, which they still occupy near
Sarre. I think these guns will surprise them a
little. At present, I conclude, from all I hear, we
are only waiting for the rains to run down and the
roads to dry a little ; and if the weather of these
last two days continue, every one says we shall
soon make a push on.

Our fellows have had a miserable time of it
lately, and when uncomfortable and idle, I am
sorry to say, they always make work for me.
We hear of daily losses, plunder, &c., and the
Spaniards perform their part well in this respect.
General O'Lalor yesterday found his secretary
had run away, down towards Madrid, with nearly
two thousand dollars, as he trusted him with every
thing. Last time I dined at head-quarters Lord
Wellington got into a long talk with me for near
two hours about the poor-laws, and the assize of

bread, about the Catholic question, the state of Ireland, &c., just as if he had nothing else upon his mind. In many points we agreed very well, particularly as to what would be necessary to be done in Ireland—if anything; but he thinks nothing should be done at all. He is still alarmed at the separation spirit which he thinks exists there, and the remains of a Jacobin feeling in the lower classes in England.

6th November.—Poor —— must pass an uncomfortable time with me here, and yet I suffer much more from having him, and he is little aware how inconvenient he is to me. In the first place, I give up one blanket of my own, and two of my servants' (who now have none), to make him a bed, and it is now very cold, and these articles are scarce, as I had just got them from Passages, and am entitled to no more for a year. Then, when I cease writing to think, I have some dull observation on the weather to answer, or on the shapes of houses, which I certainly am not a man to live here a month without finding out. To this no answer is necessary, and yet, in civility, one ought to be given, and my train of thought is broken. Then he delays my breakfast, &c., when I want to work. Next, instead of a solo in the evening with my papers, or a book, whenever I am not engaged,

I am to keep up, when tired, a dull conversation, in which I never, by any accident, pick up a new idea. The weather, however, is very fine, and we must now march soon. So ignorant, too, is he, of what are my notions, at least, of propriety, that because Lord Wellington, without being asked, has been so kind to me, and friendly in the late business, he wants me to ask him to get his brother made a Captain in the Navy! thus interfering in the patronage of a branch with which he has nothing to do, and with regard to which he is particularly scrupulous in avoiding all interference. I should just as soon think of asking him to make me Chancellor, or John Secretary of State! Yet —— is a very good sort of man, and means very well. Then comes his uncle the Colonel, now wanting to open a correspondence with me, and wishing that I should send him all the news from head-quarters, as if I had nothing else to do, at a time when I am, from necessity, neglecting almost every friend in England except your party.

To-day, 6th November, I received three letters from England. I see there is a magnificent order of the Duke of York about parcels to the army, up to a ton weight, being forwarded to officers by the Commissariat. A few such parcels would make the Commissary stare a little, when, with nearly

twelve thousand mules, we can scarcely be supplied
with bread and corn, &c., and not with forage.
You seem to know so little about the real state of
things here in England that I think the General,
who came half way up from Lisbon to review, and
then gave it up, should be employed to explain the
difficulties in the duties of office. The Commissary-general says it will take him an entire new
office, which he must write home for to keep the
accounts which this new plan will require.

Our Roncesvalles people have been terribly off;
some of the guns are buried in the snow there;
some Spaniards, as well as English have perished
by the cold, and one picket was obliged to be dug
out. I hear they are now moving away, and that
an attack by that pass must be abandoned; but we
shall soon know for certain if this dry weather
lasts. The cold increases my pains, but still, upon
the whole, braces me, and I feel better. Our
great men were all in the front, peeping to-day
into France from the mountains which surround
this hollow. Our army-post to one division, with
the dragoon carrying it, was caught two days since,
— picked up, as I was I suppose, as he had got a
little out of his way somehow; I hope no letters of
importance were caught, but it was provoking. The
French, I hear, sent back one letter to General

Oswald opened, but said the rest were all immaterial; however they did not return them. The aide-de-camp of the late Governor of Pamplona has been here for the last two days, Monsieur Pomade, a gentleman-like man; he says when the Vittoria army arrived at Pamplona on June the 24th, the garrison was three thousand strong in men, and the place provisioned for one hundred days complete, but that army, *en passant*, gave them a thousand more effective men and five hundred sick; this caused them to give in sooner than they otherwise should. He says they never expected their present fate, but that they knew nothing, and never had any communication whatever with France or Soult; that they sent out several times, but never got any one in. This is more than we can say at St. Sebastian, and does Don Carlos some credit.

The new crosses for the victories are very handsome—the medals so so, and the former will look strange with a whole row of clasps, which, I suppose Lord Wellington must have now, as he has already two, up to Salamanca, in addition to the cross. I think the thing is either too general, or not enough so, a selection of distinguished men, of all ranks, would be better than a general distribution to all of certain ranks and situations. It now shows little more than that a man had a certain rank in such a battle, and not that he performed anything more than his neighbours. A selection might have descended with advantage even to the privates. Of course many grumble, and are disappointed that others have more marks, and clasps, &c., than they have; that, however, would always be the case.

Sunday, the 6th.—Post-day for ordinary men —to-morrow for Lord Wellington; so I proceed. For the first time these fourteen months I have to-day been to a military church; I found it was indoors, and ventured, but was much reproached by my doctor; indeed they have alarmed me, as Dr. M'Gregor says, if I get cold or a bad wetting, in my present state, and with the medicines I take, I may go on crutches at Bath for two or three years. So I shall not go to church next time. We were in the newly repaired large public town room, which has just been made water and wind tight, as well as all the rooms round about it, for an hospital, and will soon, I fear, be filled with wounded. So we go on clearing away one set of hobblers, and destroying houses on both sides, then repairing and cleaning for the new set we are about to make; and then clearing off again, and so on! This town is just now clear of all the old wounded, and the large room was washed (as Dr. M'Gregor told me), though I should not have discovered it, for those soon expected, and I believe he wished not a little we had gone somewhere else to pray, and not made a dirt in his department. The service was short, plainly read, but tolerably well ; the sermon homely and familiar, but good for the troops, I think, and very fair and useful to any one. Lord Wellington was there, with his attendants, a few officers, and our new staff corps, &c.

When I returned home, lo, and behold ! I found —— very alert, waiting for breakfast, as he had orders to march on to the front in half an hour, and in less than that time, before breakfast was over, I saw Lord Wellington and his suite all off on horseback to the front, to peep again. I do not think, however, anything can be done until to-morrow, at soonest, and it will be stiffish work if the French do their duty as they ought.

I now suspect the packet will be kept until the result of what is about to be done is known, unless there is another ship ready ; my letter must, how-ever, go to-day, but I will try and send a line off if I can by the same conveyance as the despatches. As I must not go and peep, for fear of being picked up again and carried off further next time, my communications will be dull and uninteresting now. A move began to be very necessary, sickness was just commencing, and on the right, in the mountains, horses were dying fast.   If we can but beat them well we have a chance of some quiet quarter. Merely beating them back, I think, will not do for us, and if the French defend their new works with as much steadiness as they have shown activity in making them, you will have a long *Gazette*.   We all think that their *morale* is much shaken, and that the old soldiers will not stand now ; if so, the young ones will not hold out long, though it was observed that they fought best on late occasions.

———, the last thing, was at me again, about making his brother a Captain in the Navy by Lord Wellington's interest, though I thought I had sufficiently put him aside the first time, as I have no humbug in these matters.   I now was obliged to refuse him direct, telling him Lord Wellington had continually said to me, " I never interfere with the Navy, when I can help it, in any way ; I let them have all their rights, that I may keep all mine, and as I do not wish them to meddle with me, I never meddle with them."   At any rate I should never have thought of asking Lord Wellington for anything now except upon public grounds, such as repaying the Bayonne banker, &c., as it is not my doctrine that because a man has done you one favour you are therefore to ask him to do you another.

Twelve o'clock.—Six more guns are now rumbling by through this place to go up the pass; B——'s have been off some time; six more will, I hear, be soon up, and these eighteen are all to be collected to play upon the French new work, where they had yesterday got about twelve together. It is feared we must begin from the ground at too great a distance, thirteen hundred yards, but I hope closer quarters will be come to soon, as I think the French succeed best at cannonading and sharp-shooting, and we at the hand-to hand work.

Two o'clock.— The mail is said to go as usual, so I must close directly, but I have no doubt the packet will be kept, as every one says publicly the attack is to take place to-morrow morning. General Cole has just told me to go up to the top of La Rune, where I must be safe, and must see everything; I shall not go, however, unless I find all the quiet steady ones do the same, for though you may see all, and if knowing, may be down again in time, yet mistakes may be made by the unknowing, and I believe I shall remain quietly here.

Head Quarters, Vera, November 9th, 1813— I have this moment received your packet of the 26th ult., with all the kind enclosures from aunts,

cousins, &c. I shall endeavour to write to ——
this week. The week, however, may be big with
events, and I know not where, and how, this may be
finished. The attack never took place on Monday
the 8th, as I told you in my last; the roads, from
the wet, were so bad that I believe the army could
not be collected in time. To-morrow, however, is
now said to be the day, as the two last days have
continued fine and mild, the wind south, and the
thermometer up at 52° again. It now looks like
rain, but is fine and holds up as yet, with a wind
south and south-west; whilst all the rain came
with a cold north-west wind. It will not do
therefore to make use of English weather wisdom
here.

Your English mail is thought nothing of. A
Gazette of the 25th had got here first, and forestalled it; and we have to-day much greater news
from the French side, which is believed by every
one here, and by the French army as we are told;
namely, that Bony is beaten back to the Rhine, with
the loss of three divisions cut off by blowing up a
bridge too soon, &c.; one General taken, and one
drowned, &c. This puts our party in spirits for
to-morrow, and will, I hope, damp the French if
believed by them, as the deserters, &c., report
it to be.

The Portuguese are most anxious to enter France, and are in high spirits ; the grave ones, however, expect a great number of broken heads, unless the French turn tail shamefully. You ask me about Baron de Trengueléon, and if I thought of him whilst I was a prisoner. I certainly did at Mont de Marsan, and inquired and found I was within thirty miles of him ; and an emigrant there advised me to apply to go over to see him, but I thought it might do us both harm, and therefore, never said a word upon the subject to any one. Major D—— had serious thoughts of going as my servant with the baggage to look about ; but it would have been a dangerous experiment.

To all my numberless kind inquirers, pray return my best thanks: to write to them myself is impossible.

The 10*th November.*—I dined with Lord Wellington last night, and staid there till near ten. He was all gaiety and spirits ; and only said on leaving the room, " Remember ! at four in the morning." Monsieur Pomade, the governor of Pamplona's aide-de-camp, was there, and I sat next to him, and had some conversation. He had been told operations were going on, and that that was the reason he could be not sent in yet to the French. To show what he expected to be the result, he told me (when I begged him to tell the banker at Bayonne that all his letters had been sent safe) that except from necessity and orders he should avoid Bayonne, as he was not ready yet to be shut up again in another town.

To-day every one was in motion here two hours before daylight; and the cavalry passed, part of them, through here at five o'clock. I got up, and had all packed ready, and breakfast, &c., by daylight, and found every one was gone to see the glorious attack—even the doctors and the two parsons : so I determined to venture up to the top of La Rune in the way General Cole recommended. The day was beautiful. I passed the camp of the latter in my way up, and should have heard there of any check. I then pursued my way, and staid on the top from about eight until two, hearing and seeing fire and smoke all the way along the hills from St. Jean de Luz to near St. Jean Pied de Port. The whole was visible at once; and I could see the men even with the naked eye, by the glitter of their arms for a considerable way. The French redoubts crowned the tops of all their positions with deep ditches, &c.; and they had full shelter in woods and houses, &c.; but our fellows slowly beat them on and on, from place to place, and forced their way until all the right of the position seemed ours. Two redoubts on the hill below me I saw abandoned shamefully, when our fellows got round them. A large star fort on the top took more time. The men from the others tried to make for it, but failed ; though mostly got off on our side. Those in the fort I left surrounded by our men, who ran up in four or five directions to within about fifty yards or less, firing as they ran ; and then bobbed all down for shelter until all were ready. They lay in this way nearly an hour. When satisfied that the men shut up must be prisoners (as I hear they were) I returned home.

On the ridge of hills all along the right, the rows of fired huts added not a little to the scene. By whom burnt I know not. The cannon roared away in the mountains. On the hill, amongst others, I met Lord E. Somerset, the cavalry General, gone up to look out, with Colonel Vivian and Mr. Heaphy. He was there before me, when the fighting was nearer, and declares he saw one English soldier bayonet two French officers who attacked him when advanced from the others—first one and then the other. I hope our loss has not been severe, considering what the position was.

I believe we were to have moved to Sarré ; but General Giron has taken seventy houses there for

his staff; and the rest are full of wounded. I
think, from what I have heard, our officers think
themselves well out of the scrape. The left of our
army towards St. Jean de Luz was refused;—that
is the French were not pressed there much, in
hopes of forming the right so rapidly, as to cut off
a good lot on the left. I do not think that will
be the case, but that they must move off to night
to a new position, and not having such another
line of works, the French must stand to-morrow if
attacked openly on the hills, or run for it. I have
seen no one yet, so only give you my own views,
which may be probably very wide of the *Gazette*.
It was a terrible fag for my new mare, and at top
cool, and no room to walk about; I have in consequence, a new fidget in her refusing her food.
A little English hay I still have left, will, I hope,
tempt her to try some corn. The troops will de-
vour all the forage in front, and I do not know how
we shall get on at all. I am now about to buy
another pony; but the movements stop all other
arrangements. The pains in my bones are at present, I think, better for my ride and walk, and
a spare dinner on a tough mutton chop, on my
return I was rather afraid of the cold wind on
the top of La Rune; but do not as yet feel at all
the worse, but am excessively tired, and must go

to bed though only eight o'clock, as I was up at four, and awake at three. So adieu.

Head-Quarters, St. Fé, November 12, 1813.— At seven, yesterday morning, we got orders to march; all the baggage to assemble at Sarré, and wait there for orders. We did so; and on our way crossed the first French redoubts and positions, and began to see our wounded and the stripped dead lying about as usual. So starved and weak were many of the animals, and so clayey and deep the roads, that the scene had almost the appearance of a retreat, except that we passed all the wounded and prisoners going to the rear, instead of marching with them. The Spanish oxen were so starved, and thin, and weak, that in the first league I think I counted about eleven lying down to die, whilst every now and then a serjeant with his pike, or a soldier gave them a stab, half out of humanity, and half to see the effect, and from a sort of love of fun. Then there were ten or fifteen poor women belonging to the baggage of the division lamenting over their dying donkeys and mules, whilst others were brutally beating some to death, because they would not go farther. In every direction baggage was falling off, and the whole formed a glorious scene of confusion. Near Sarré I was caught in a violent storm, but got to a

house for shelter before I was wet, and there stood
in the doorway of a deserted house, with three
dead bodies on the ground close by; one was certainly an officer, from his clean skin, and neatly-
shaven beard, and whiskers, and from every remnant of his dress having been worth stealing. The
other two were Spaniards.

The Spaniards behaved tolerably in the field,
but not like the fourth division and the light, &c.
They excelled them, however, in plunder and mischief. I found them breaking and plundering one
of the best houses in Sarré when I was there. Our
own people are grown expert hands, and Lord Wellington threatens hanging, and, I believe, has hung
a few in vain. The people in general have fled,
and the Spaniards come in to carry off pots, pans,
dishes, chairs, tables, &c., &c., to refurnish their
own houses. At Sarré, I found the civil departments were to stay there, and the military to come
on to this place. My baggage had gone by in part
before I knew this ; and, besides that I could no-
where find a house. The Spaniards were in possession, and firing, plunder, and confusion was all
around ; I determined, therefore, to come on here.
and take my chance.

You all advise me to keep well in the rear for
safety ; I can only say the most knowing ones (in

which opinion I agree) consider the rear as the most unsafe place of any. All the vagabonds, plunderers, and rascals, followers of the army, stick to the rear, and look about to do mischief as soon as all the troops are passed. Besides which it is not clear here that the peasants, who all fly, may not return, and knock a few on the head, though at present they seem terrified and excessively alarmed. I found no quarters for me here, but at a little village close by, where there were only the Commissary-general and a few of his deparment, I took possession of a deserted house, which had been ransacked, cleaned it out a little in one place, and finding abundance of food left for my horses for two or three nights, thought myself well off, though I was somewhat alarmed at having possession of the last inhabited house on that road, from the fear of any straggling attack, or the owners coming back in the night. There was, however, no alternative. All the immediately useful part of my baggage was behind, and never arrived at all, having been turned out of the road by a Spanish division. Unluckily, my neighbours were nearly in the same state. Sir Robert Kennedy had barely enough for his own eating, and went to bed leaving his servants to do the best they could.

H—— had nothing : baggage not arrived. Mr.

H——n had one half loaf, and that served us all
Mr. M——, the storekeeper, had got some mutton
for Lord Wellington to-day, and he spared us a little
bit each ; so I got one mutton chop, and was very
lucky, or I should have dined on a knuckle bone
of pork (which I was boiling whilst Henry was
looking for the baggage), having found this morsel
on the top of the bed. I then laid down half un-
dressed to try and sleep, but was not very well
and got but little rest.

Between four and five, Henry went to inquire
about marching, and, finding no orders, we remained
quiet. About seven or eight, he found my two
stray mules, and I got a loaf of bread and some
potted butter out of my stock, and went and
made my contribution to the party, which was
very acceptable. I have since been down to head-
quarters to know what is going on; but can learn
nothing except that we are ready now to cross the
Nivé, and are prepared for that step ; particulars I
can hear none, as only the clergyman, the doctors,
and a straggling civilian, with the Provost guard,
are to be seen.

I returned, therefore, to my deserted desolate
home to wash, and shave, and get the mud
cleared off my boots ; and took to this occupation
of writing to you, though rather feverish and un-

comfortable. I must get a stewed beef-steak early, and go to bed at eight to night, to recover for to-morrow. In my way I found one of the owners of a house here who had been shot through the thigh by a Portuguese; I got him to an hospital to be dressed, in the church, where French, English, and all were lying to wait their turn, with now and then a dead one. As soon as they are dressed, they are packed off to the rear on mules, &c. So we go on!

The famous French bulletin has now been seen. Some say Bony is at Paris, and some think he will come here. Others have a notion the people beyond Bayonne are ready to join us, if we proceed on. I fear, however, the runaways will not encourage this much with their exaggerated stories of our conduct in their villages. To-day is a very fine day again, and will, I hope, assist our operations much. I hear that when our officers went up to the men in the star fort, to call upon them to surrender, the Colonel commanding said, like the governor of Pamplona, "Yes, on the terms of parole, not to serve for a year and a day." "No, no," says the Englishman; "*prisonnier.*" "*Eh bien, donc je ne me rends pas,*" says the French-man. "But you must and shall, or you will all be murdered," says the Englishman, and then turned

away. Upon which the Colonel very sulkily
returned and consented ; and when his soldiers
rather began to rejoice, and to quiz the *ré papé*,
and say, dancing about, that it was time it should
all end, he was most indignantly sulky, and has
remained so ever since, complaining of being sent
off to England as a prisoner.

I have now under my window a characteristic
scene. A short Portuguese lad, bloated out with
ration beef, with an old French helmet on, and a
great red grenadier's feather, and an old French
uniform jacket and pantaloons, with a dragoon
broadsword, cutting down cabbages and apples in
the garden for his brother Portuguese, who has
his apron ready to receive them, whilst a dirty,
brown, snuff-coloured Spaniard is looking about
on the other side with an old French musket
trying to shoot something eatable.

The mixture of the silence of a deserted village
with the occasional riotous noise of muleteers and
stragglers, Portuguese and Spaniards, as well as a
few swearing English, is striking ; but to a person
not actively engaged in what is going on, by which
all minor considerations vanish in the dangers and
anxiety of the scene, there is a sameness of misery
and starvation, of wounds, and of death, which
when the novelty of the scene is over becomes very

unpleasant, especially without any rational companion to talk to on what is passing.   I suspect I
am in the house of a curé, as there are the remains
of many comforts, and of some books chiefly re-
ligious, some crosses, &c., &c.

I just now met a man who spoke English tolerably, and French well, but would address me in
Spanish, to say the people were plundering all the
flour at the only mill in the place which was at
work, and he requested a guard, and wanted the
Commandant.   I luckily saw the feather of the
Superintendent of the Provost guard entering a
house opposite, and got him a guard directly.   So
that one can be of some use without meddling
much.

I have just now had a Spaniard at my door to
know how he could get back safe to Spain, as he
had wandered here alone, and dared not return,
and had nothing to eat.   I have sent him off with
a small bit of bread and a shilling, and advised
him to go and remain near the Provost guard, and
keep with the first escort of prisoners which sets
out for Spain.

Nearly all the houses about me are empty, and
I do not much like my situation, but it is just now
like a wife, for better, for worse ; so I must submit.
I do not think we have a hundred men within

three miles, and not one soldier within half a mile, only commissaries, and young doctors, and a stray shot fired every three or four minutes. My own muleteers I have just stopped.

November 13*th.*—Here I am still in my solitary abode. It has rained all night I am sorry to say, and the roads are running water-courses, which will I fear impede our progress. All, I hear, however, is going on well. I have not seen a creature, or been out ; only sent to the Commissary-general, my neighbour, to ascertain, we are not to march for fear I should be left behind here. Several of the elderly owners of houses have returned, but mine has not. Lord Wellington has ordered what forage, &c., can be regularly used, and collected, to be paid for punctually, and I understand has determined to send back at least a part of the Spaniards, on account of their abominable conduct, Longa's people in particular. I cannot be surprised at it, but it spoils all our plans. We were admitted quietly into St. Jean de Luz, and the inhabitants remained there. The mayor offered to exert himself to get what he could collected, to supply the troops regularly ; and Sir John Hope flogged the two first men he caught taking some wine—this instantly ; so I hope that town will be preserved.

We can never do well if we go on driving all the population before us. The few old people left here, and who are coming in, speak only Basconee and a little Gascon, and no French. There is no making them understand anything.

To-day would have been dreadful up in the mountains, so we have at least that reflection to comfort ourselves with. I send enclosed Lord Wellington's letter to me and Count Gazan's. Pray keep the former, as I shall always value it.

4 o'clock, afternoon, November 13*th.*—It has been raining so incessantly ever since morning, that I have not stirred from my hole, and have, therefore, seen no one ; but I understand all the grandees were to have gone to the front at five this morning, but from the state of the weather, they have all stopped at home, not for the fear of a wetting themselves, but I conclude from the impossibility of getting through the country, and across rivers, when in such a state. I only wonder how ur men got on, as they did up the hills on the 12th. It was as much as I could do with my horse singly on a slippery clay, either so hard, a horse could not stand on it, or so deep, he was up to his knees, between the hard places. We are now, however, almost fairly out of the Pyrenees, and I hope our roads will mend, but from what I saw of the high road, I doubt it. I have been pacing the room, sweeping, and chopping wood for exercise.

November 14*th*.—Still here at St. Fé, as I find the place is called, now I have had a peep at an excellent old French map the Commissary-general has got from the Mayor. Still rain, and nothing new, except that the French have been well frightened, and mean as we are told to quit their new position which they have taken, with their left on Bayonne, as soon as it is attacked ; that is, as soon I conclude as the roads will let us move. The communications here are almost as bad as in Spain, from hence to St. Jean de Luz almost impassable. The Marquis of Worcester, I have just heard, goes to-day, in an hour.

Head Quarters, St. Jean de Luz, November 24*th*, 1813.—Having a little leisure, I must begin my weekly journal. As to health, I am upon the whole much better ; our weather continues beautiful, and I generally get my hour's walk, and my hour's ride daily. Some prog vessels have also arrived from England, and this gives us a few comforts. Some things we were before almost without, light in particular, as bad candles were 12*s.* a pound, and very scarce. A Dartmouth brig sold off an immense stock of good English moulds yesterday, in the morning at 2s. 6d. a pound, by order from head-quarters, and about five tons of potatoes, besides quantities of porter, ale, beef, cheese, &c. The scramble of officers on board to see and buy would have astonished you not a little. We have also some good white wine.

Since our move from the mountains our men are all behaving much better : they were becoming very bad, I suppose from a sort of despair. Desertion, even from the English to the French, was frequent. The temptation of the " old gentleman" in the high mountains was too much for the men. It has now almost entirely ceased. I hope, therefore, when we are a little quiet, and my arrears are cleared off, that I shall have much less to do. Our reports here now are that Bonaparte's aide-de-camp is at Bayonne, and that he himself is expected. If so we may probably have some work to do here again, unless he has been obliged merely to show himself here to convince his army that he is still alive and well.

We had a little affair yesterday. Some of the light division were ordered to drive in the French pickets in one place where they were too forward, and our men being too zealous, pushed too far. In trying to prevent this, a fine officer of the 43rd was taken, and a lieutenant badly wounded, and

some men lost. The only annoyance I suffer at
present in my quarters arises from the multiplicity
of inhabitants, namely, three old women, seven
children, three dogs, two cats, and a fair allowance
of fleas, whom this late fine weather has revived.
We have lately had an arrival at Passages of a
hundred and fifty oxen from Ireland for the army,
and are promised the same supply weekly. This
will do something ; but our consumption is, I believe, about a thousand a week. Our forage in
this nook of France is as bare as in the neighbouring parts of Spain ; every field is eaten close down,
and all straw of corn and maize consumed. I sent
twelve miles for straw yesterday, and the mules
have returned to-day empty. I mean now to try
bruised furze, to mix with their Indian corn, so as
to hold out until some more hay shall reach us
from England.

November 25.—I have just heard that about
two thousands of our inhabitants returned here last
night, but Soult would not suffer them to carry
much with them.

November 26.—I had time for no more yesterday, and to-day I have nothing to add. I have
still not received or heard anything from you
later than the 3rd, but we have papers here to
the 13th. I cannot understand how this has

occurred. Through France we have news still later, and have heard of the surrender of Davoust's corps at Hamburg, on terms of not serving for a year and a day. I only hope the terms may be kept. I had a droll *malheur* again to-day. Riding my pony into the sea, into about six inches water to wash his legs, a wave came, the sand gave way, and he sunk up to his middle, so that my legs were half up to the calf in sand. I jumped off, and went over his head to run out, as I feared he could not rise. We thus both got safely out, the poor pony much more frightened than I was.

I conclude everything goes on well, as Lord Wellington and his gentlemen were to-day out with the hounds. He told me that I kept him up reading Courts-martial until twelve o'clock at night or one in the morning; and this every night. I hope, however, this will not last long. The Prince of Orange has got a complaint in his eyes, but I believe only a cold, and he seems better. Nearly all our great men except Lord Wellington have been ill.

Send me some law news, and good, for Lord Wellington expects me to tell him who all the new judges are to be, &c., and is very fond of discussing legal subjects. At first I was generally

right in my speculations : but I have now no
means of knowing how things are going on unless
you keep up my credit ; it must not be, however,
by loose reports.

I have a poor young Commissary B——, under
charges, who has, I think, been very ill used by a
Spanish alcalde. I fought his battle with Lord
Wellington to-day to get him released from arrest.
He is very well spoken of, and said to support his
two sisters. Can he be a brother of the Miss
B——'s, you know ? I detected the Spanish
General F—— in a little bit of a fib on this subject. His excuse for not answering my letter for
eight days was, that it had been delayed in the
post. I complained, and his receipt for the letter
was produced the day after it was sent — this on
the back of the cover.

Sunday, November 29.— Still no news, and no
accounts from England. We are all anxiety. I
am just come from church at the drum-head, on
the sands by the sea. Two brigades of guards
present in their best, and white trousers, &c., and
Lord Wellington and his staff here. It was rather
cold work. The weather is beginning to change
again I fear for rain, just as the roads were becoming passable. You have no conception how
soon fifteen thousand sharp-footed heavy-laden

mules, in rain, cut up a road in this country, even when at first tolerably good. We have been amused with Cobbet's attributing all Bonaparte's misfortunes to his being grafted into the old stock. If he can now manage well he may, I think, still get his little king Pepin graft to thrive in France, and beat Mr. Knight and our gardeners. The true cause of all is, however, that the *morale* of the people of Europe is changed. It was France, army and people, against mere armies and bad governments, whilst all the people in Europe were indifferent at the least. This is now reversed; and it is now a mere French army against every people and army; and Frenchmen at least quite indifferent.

CHAPTER VII.

NEWS FROM FRANCE—LORD FITZROY SOMERSET—DEPARTURE
OF THE PRINCE OF ORANGE—EXCHANGE OF PRISONERS—
PROXIMITY OF THE TWO ARMIES—WELLINGTON'S COOKS—
WARLIKE MOVEMENTS—FRENCH ATTACK—THE GUARDS—
DESERTERS—MORE FIGHTING.

> Head-Quarters, St. Jean de Luz,
> December 2, 1813.

MY DEAR M——

AT last we have got a mail from England.
Your papers give us little public news, that is, news
to us, as you have no late accounts from the Allies,
and French papers we always get sooner this
way. Thus we have long known of Bonaparte's
arrival at Paris, which you only just now communicate to us. Lord Wellington has, I understand, news of a rising in Holland ; and this has
been confirmed by our reports through the French,
who, in conversation with Dashwood yesterday,
when he went in with a flag of truce, and a parcel
of women, seemed to admit it. We had had this

as a report before the arrival of the packet, and
Major Dashwood therefore tried to pump them
on the subject. We have also had a report here
that Admiral Young had taken the Texel fleet ;
but as no news of this sort has reached us from
you, we fear from dates that this must be all false.

This is only a Passages report from some straggling ships, not French news. The deserters who
come in also from Bayonne, &c., and the returned
inhabitants, all state that the Italian regiments
here have been removed to the rear ; at least all
Italian officers have given up their lodgings and
have packed up. I think now they will scarcely
rely much upon the Dutch either, and there were
some fine men and several good officers of that
nation here. I believe I told you that the only
two officers who were disinterested, and most uni-
formly civil to us whilst we were prisoners, were
two Dutchmen of the 130th regiment.

The Burgundy side of France (Switzerland being
with us) is certainly as unguarded as this frontier,
except by a naturally strong country in places.
Strasburg, the only strong place almost except our
old friends Huningen and Kehl, is far removed,
and the latter may be left on one side, I should
think ; but for all this the French Italian army
must be well disposed of first.

If Lord Charles Somerset deserves promotion as
well as our Military Secretary here, the grumbling
you mention against his appointment must be
unfounded. That is all I can say, and I know
nothing more. The latter gets through a great
amount of business with little assistance, and always
quite in public, almost in a common coffee or
lounging room, in the midst of talking, noise, joking,
and confusion. The Prince of Orange left us yesterday. As he used to be one of the above loungers,
this put me in mind of him. He has had a complaint in his eyes, and could not embark before
yesterday, when he did so with a fair wind. His
arrival, however, and all news about him will pre-
cede this. The French, yesterday, when told that
he was going off for England, said, "Oh they
supposed it was in consequence of what had happened in Holland." In short, the French seem still
(as when I was in France and now even more so)
willing to listen to all bad news against Bonaparte,
and do not make the least of it at all. All exchange
of officers, &c , here has now, I fear, at last been
broken off, and angry letters have passed. How
fortunate I was ! I will send in your French Captain
Le Feivre's letter concerning his exchange, if an
opportunity should offer soon, and it is permitted.

Friday, December 3rd.—I find Lord Wellington's Dutch insurrection news came to him by a telegraphic note from Mr. Croker, dated the 20th ult. This is a grand point. Next for Italy, and then we shall do ; and after twenty-three years of murder, we have a reasonable chance of being able to give the military word when things go wrong, —" As you were."

The Prince of Orange, from all appearances here, where the sea has been tremendous, must have had a most famous passage ; but I should think a quick one, as the wind has been fair. We have a notion that he has been chased by four French frigates which have escaped from some French port. I yesterday gave a grand dinner at the French Café here ; the dinner was abundant, and from the paucity of materials the variety was surprising. Ten dishes for the first course, two re- moves for the soups ; ten for the second course, rotis and sweets together ; ten for desert ; and we were ten in company, and two excuses—dinner for twelve. Some dishes were admirable, particularly all the patisseries. The champaign excellent ; Madeira and sherry very fair ; port and claret very moderate. I am now paying the bill, and the *tout ensemble* is forty dollars.

I spoke to Lord Wellington this morning about the French Captain's letter you sent to me. He laughed and said, "Yes, when you can, you may send it; but the whole matter is now at an end, and your companions are all sent to the rear, as Bonaparte has refused to let the exchanges take place, unless three French go for one British, one Spaniard, and one Portuguese—the old squabble in Mackenzie's negociation, and though very flattering to us as English, very unpleasant to our poor prisoners."

We have a most tremendous sea here—now worse than ever. The waves at high water break every time almost over an old wall about twenty feet high on the beach, and come over the stone walk; they roar most furiously, and are beyond anything I have ever seen. A Paymaster here declares he saw a brig go down, and disappear instantly about nine or ten o'clock yesterday near Andaye. We shall be long, I fear, before we hear again from you in England. I do not think any ships will venture near us now, certainly not to Passages or here.

Post-day, Sunday, 5th December.—Our storms have now subsided, and the sea gets calmer; but the mischief already known has been considerable. The vessel I mentioned above that was seen to sink, I believe got at last into the Bidassoa, but four transports I hear have been lost in Passages

harbour and several lives. One vessel drove into
a house and knocked it down; most of the shipping there is damaged, and many of the boats
crushed between them. An English merchant-
vessel also went down at the entrance of Bayonne,
as we are told. The air is now colder, almost
frosty, and a dry wind; mountains all covered
with snow; I only hope this may last. No more
news from you, and we are here in a very odd
state—I mean that our armies are. A few years
back in Spain, the British were uneasy, when a
French army patrolled within thirty miles of them.
Now we have all got quietly into quarters—are
nearly all housed; and three-fourths of us go to
sleep tranquilly every night, and our front is within
sixty yards of the French.

Colonel S—— tells me he went to breakfast
with Colonel H—— the Assistant Adjutant-
general of the sixth division at Ustaritz, and there
they were in a house with their breakfast-table
within about fifty yards of the French sentry, and
within about two hundred of the whole French
picket, who by one volley might have broken all
their cups and saucers, if not their heads. The
other day a Portuguese brigade had a field-day
close to the river in the meadows, and all the
French came down to look at them, and I have no

doubt from the general report, to admire and
approve ; whilst on the other hand, in the meadows
on the French side, the French conscripts are
brought down to be drilled, sometimes five or six
squads are seen at once, and any one of the sar-
jeants might be knocked on the head all the time
by our sentries ; but this is now all well understood,
and we thus quietly bully or bravado each other.

Another party of inhabitants have come in here
—women and children ; the men Soult detains.
We shall thus add to our female stock, and to the
seven hundred Portuguese women and four hundred
Spanish, who are already in this place and the
environs as settlers, *vivanderos*, washerwomen, &c.
In short, here we are in quiet winter quarters, for
a time at least, with head-quarters within seven
miles of the French, and yet we are all so at our
ease, even in France, that the baggage animals of
head-quarters are gone now beyond Tolosa, forty
miles and more to the rear, for straw to feed the
horses. Lord Wellington told me yesterday there
was no forage left here ; and I suppose no army so
large ever staid so long in these mountains. But
yet, if a spring campaign comes, I have no doubt
we shall, somehow or other, find all our animals
forthcoming, and in a state for service.

The Irish oxen sent out for the Commissariat

have proved very good, excellent in comparison, and are served out as a *bonne bouche*—a pound or two with five or six of the country beef. In short, we have lately, now and then, had the London alderman's cry of more fat ; and for a novelty a gentleman is asked if he likes fat, and sends his plate for it. Without joking, Lord Wellington's table is now very good in every respect ; and I think his aides-de-camp will be ill with excess, who have this daily fare (unless there is a move), especially if the roads remain too bad for exercise. Lord Wellington has now three cooks, and an English and Spanish chief share the command, and by dividing the days, vie with each other.

More rain—more rain,—I am sorry to say ! I have just seen Lord Wellington ; he is much annoyed. A poor Commissary under charges has fallen sick. I reported that he was at Passages, too ill to move to be tried, and that I have two certificates of medical men of the necessity of his going to England. Lord Wellington told me to tell the Adjutant-general not to let him get away ; and that if he remained too ill to move, we must try him at Passages. It was for violent conduct to another Commissary. I have no time to add more.

Head-Quarters, St. Jean de Luz, December 8th,

1813.—A packet is just arrived, and I have letters
from you of the 22nd ult., and papers to the same
date. Letters and papers are, however, here by
the same vessel to the 25th. A most remarkable
and astonishing paper!

     *   *   *   *

I hope this fine weather will give us some hay
from England, as I have now nothing for forage
but furze and bran, which I buy to give my animals
by way of hay.

I have had by this packet a long letter from
——; they want me to ask for Captain ——'s
promotion. I am determined not to ask favours,
even if I supposed it would be of any use. I hope
I have just saved one promising young officer by
getting him to make, and another to accept, an
apology, and Lord Wellington to agree to this.
He would otherwise on trial have been broken, I
believe. My letter, ordering the Court to meet,
was taken by the French; and this gave time,
and opened a long correspondence, which has given
me much trouble, which, however, I shall not
grudge if it ends well. I have scribbled this over
my pint of good sherry, which I have got from a
suttler, who has brought it here all the way from
Madrid by land. I must now go and prepare
charges against a German doctor for to-morrow,

and against two Portuguese for a highway robbery.
So adieu.

Thursday, 9th.—All peaceable business has
ceased ; and here I am in an enemy's town quite
at ease. All the troops advanced about four this
morning, and we have here only a Provost guard
of about forty men, a few straggling guards, and
the muleteers, servants and civilians. The French
dared not to have remained so in Spain, in any
town, much more in Portugal.

I went out to my morning's walk on the beach.
I had it to myself nearly, and heard a sharp firing
of both guns, and particularly musketry, sounding
quite close to us. Our present object is, I believe,
merely to move up our right, as we are much
pinched in our present position. We are now with
our right at Itoasso, Espellette, and Cambo, on
the Nivé ; our centre at Ustaritz and St. Fé ; and
our left by Bidart, Ahetze, and Arbonne, all on
the Spanish or south side of the Nivé. Our object
now is to move up the right, nearly or quite to the
Adour, I believe, only making a feint at Biarits
and Anglet, near Bayonne, on the left, unless good
fortune puts more in our power. We shall then
be more at ease, cover more ground, and open a
little country on the right for our cavalry to get
quarters and accommodation, at least that part

which is still with us in front. This, I believe, is all the intended present plan.

Should the report of the French mayor here prove correct, or the deputy mayor rather, as the chief is off, namely, that there is an insurrection at Bordeaux, and that the Allies are within fifty leagues of Paris, it may soon be *autre chose ;* but at present we are only, as I hear, taking elbow-room for winter-quarters, and putting ourselves in a position to start when advisable. We shall also see how the French are disposed to fight, and judge a little what forces are gone to the rear. How angry it made me to see your nonsensical reports of our being not only in Bayonne, but in Bordeaux, and this given out formally at the play-house ! To exaggerate just now is so unnecessary, so unreasonable, and so injurious to those who do so much !

Three o'Clock.—The firing has continued more or less the whole day, but is now more distant, and the great guns near Bayonne are heard occasionally. As yet, however, no news, except from a wounded Guardsman, just come in, shot in the hand, who says the Guards are advancing and the French retreating,—I conclude into their lines opposite Bayonne. A fleet of twelve sail, or perhaps fifteen, in sight. Hurrah ! for hay and money, we all say !

The army is only paid up to May, and the staff to April. I have to-day commenced a fire, having a little cold, and being rather more rheumatic ; upon the whole, however, I am better. It rained much in the night, which was against our movements, but has nearly held up since, though it has just dropped all day.

Friday, the 10*th.*—Lord Wellington did not return last night, nor the Adjutant-general and grandees. I hear but little except that we crossed the Nivé well on the right, but did not make much progress in the course of the day. On our left we did rather more than I expected, and I am told pushed on to within a mile of Bayonne, with some loss ; so we rested last night, and we have had constant showers, at times very heavy, ever since. This is very much against our arrangements.

Four o'clock.—Here I have remained quiet all day, but in a fidget, as from eleven o'clock there has been continually firing in our front, and of course, though within six or seven miles of us, we have had all sorts of reports, some rather alarming, to me at least, as I believe Lord Wellington is on the other side of the Nivé, with our right, and I have not the same confidence in any one else, especially as only a part of our army is on this side the river. The communication is troublesome, and the

French have evidently made a push here to-day in force, whilst our brigades are all separated. The Guards came back here last night to their positions and quarters, and the 5th division to Bidart and its environs. Some Caçadores were surprised and some prisoners made, and the French showed themselves in force in this line, and have, I believe, pushed us back to our old ground before the troops could be collected again.

At two o'clock the firing was so loud, and so near in appearance, that I began to see about my baggage, especially as an order came from the Guards here to turn out again and advance. I have, however, just seen the Commissary-general, Sir R. Kennedy, and he says there is no danger, as he left the French checked by our works on our old position, and met four brigades on the road advancing to assist. He was, however, a little surprised himself, at the end of his ride, to see what was going on, as suddenly a fire began across the road where he was looking, near our cavalry, and when he turned about, our guns began across the other way, and he was obliged to sneak off. One never can be quite secure in these attacks.

I am told a note was taken from the French General Gautier to the Duke of Dalmatia, sent to tell him a deserter had come in from us at two

o'clock, and told him of the intended attack yesterday, and complaining much of desertions on his
side. It is very provoking, that our fellows should
always betray us in this manner; but it seems to
have been of no consequence.

St. Jean de Luz, Head-Quarters, December 11*th,*
1813.—From what I hear to-day, there were some
grounds for my uneasiness yesterday, but only slight
ones. The French, as I told you, made a bold push
with nearly four divisions on the high road. We
had only one division, or I believe only part of one
at hand ready. Some Portuguese in advance were
surprised, and lost prisoners and baggage. The
French regained all they had lost the day before.
At about two o'clock they made a push at our
position. A Portuguese brigade suffered very
much, and I am told dispersed. An English bri-
gade·also is said to have been unlike the rest of
late : that is all I can say. Lord Wellington had
heard the firing and received intelligence of the
attack; he came across the river Nivé instantly,
and halted the sixth division on this side, which
was going over by former orders to act on the
other, on the right. The 4th was ordered up
to support the light division. Lord Wellington
himself was foremost in trying to rally the Portuguese, &c.; both he and his staff were much ex-

posed, and had not often, as I hear, been in a warmer fire.

The French were induced to attack our redoubt and position by their successes and numbers. Our reinforcements came up ; they were repulsed, driven back with loss, and I think our ground, which we had already gained and lost once, was nearly all ours again last night, at the close of day. They talk of a thousand wounded, probably more, on our part. We have taken some prisoners, and many wounded French ; at one time, however, a whole regiment of Portuguese, and some English also, were nearly being made prisoners. The Guards, or as they are called here " the gentlemen's sons," were too late, as they had so far to march. They, in fact, have not seen, this campaign, anything like so much fire as I have, and will never learn their trade of being killed properly if they are thus nursed up in the rear. Their great grievance at present is the order about horses and mules, limiting the numbers to the old regulations, on account of forage, and I believe allowing subaltern officers only their one animal, so that if they ride they cannot carry anything. If they carry baggage they must walk, and then when they come into their quarters, and their real duty towards the men com- mences, they are unfit for anything. The regulation is, therefore, a severe one, and most think it over-does the thing.

On the other hand, the present establishment of the Guards is absolutely ridiculous. Every subaltern officer has his two or three horses, and his three or four mules, as much as any staff-officer ought to have. He carries his bed out to the guard-house, or picket, and has his canteen fit to give a dinner, and every luxury, &c. ; whereas one set of canteens, &c., per company, would be a liberal allowance, I think. Their General has given them six weeks to comply with this order, but somehow or other they will contrive, I think, to evade it, or they will be the most miserable animals in exist-ence. Whilst they were in camp, they left one officer with the men in camp, and the rest got into houses, whilst in many instances at that time even the Generals in other divisions commanding bri-gades, were out under canvass (then in the moun-tains), or at most in huts. Both men and officers are only fit for our old style of expedition,— a landing, a short march, and a good fight, and then a lounge home again. The men were yesterday all sore-footed with their march, but at church last Sunday, in their white linen pantaloons, they looked in high order ; and the appearance of the men, the care of their dress, their discipline and general good conduct, is admirable when in quiet quarters here.

I met young ——, an Ensign in the Guards, yesterday, a son of Lord —— —. He is a very gentleman-like stripling of nineteen, talks of just remembering Sir John Moore's death, as the beginning of his political knowledge, and something about General Castanos, and the first Spanish publication of Cevallos, but is quite in a wilderness when you talk of the old state of Europe before the French Revolution. He now principally talks of the table, and who gives best wines and dinners, and found fault with General ——'s, which I must say appeared to me most luxurious, and reminded me of fine dinners in London.

10 *o'clock.*—Hurrah! hurrah! I have just been called out to see three small battalions of deserters pass by with drums beating, and colours flying, with their arms and everything in the highest condition, and clothing nearly new. Two battalions of the regiment De Nassau, and one of the regiment De Frankfort, in the whole twelve hundred men. This is a grand consequence of our push, and must alarm the French not a little. I should not be surprised now if we advance soon, whatever might have been our former plans. Lord Wellington was out again in the front this morning, up at three

and out in the dark. He returns to dinner to-day, and has invited the German Colonels and the Majors, six of them, to dinner, to which he means to return. He has also desired they may now have their breakfasts, &c.: the whole remain in quarters here for the night, and proceed to-morrow for Passages I presume, though it is several miles off, as the Spaniards occupy all the places between (except Irun, which is voted unwholesome and feverish), and will scarcely give a quarter to an English officer, and not to our detachments coming up to join (who have to march through here always); so I conclude they would not do more for the Germans who have once served with the French. The only drawback to these good things is the thought of the poor wounded, crawling in, on foot, or on cars, and on mules, crying with the pain of the motion. It is now quite fine, and I must go to my sea promenade; so for the present adieu.

Later, the 11*th.*—Our Major D——- has found a friend in the Colonel of the regiment which came over, and who has told him how it happened and was managed. An officer from the North had found the way to him (the Colonel) all through France, with an order from his real sovereign to go over to us, and come and join him. He communicated his plan to no one but the Major (one Major).

They waited their opportunity, and when it arose
last night, he called the officers together, told them
his order and his resolution, and proposed it to
them, but said he should force no one ; it must be
voluntary.   All agreed—and the men were too
happy to join in the plan.   One officer was sent in
to give us notice and to clear the way, and to prevent any resistance or confusion.   He was also to
make terms that they were not to be compelled to
serve, &c.   The officer, however, did not like going
back, and before any message was sent, over they
all came.   On their arrival here to-day, just out of
the town, they halted, and put on their best clothes
to pass through in parade order, and very well
they looked I assure you.   They say there are
many Spanish, and two good regiments of cavalry
who would come over probably, if a pardon were
held out to them, and that there are a number of
Dutch all ready to do the same thing, but they are
principally officers, and are not in a body.   They
are tumultuous and troublesome, and only wait the
proper occasion.

The Colonel, K——, has written to Marshal
Soult telling him why he came over—that he was
ordered so to do, &c., and after reminding him that
as long as they were French, and he with the
French, he had done his duty.   In return, he

193

requests (and rather an impudent request I think it is), that the women and the baggage, or at least the baggage soldiers and servants, may be allowed to join the regiments. He also asks that his band, which he says was excellent, as it was his hobby-horse, and which was of course left behind, may be allowed to join the rest. Of this however he has no hopes, as his band was always a subject of considerable jealousy to the French before he left them, and he is sure they will keep it now for themselves.

I also hear our staff officers were obliged to exert themselves very much in consequence of the dispersion of the Portuguese, and the reluctance of some of our own forces. Colonel Delancey took one colour, and rode on before the regiments to carry them on. General Hope was much exposed, and got two blows, one on the shin, and one on his side, but of no consequence. General Pakenham had a horse shot under him—his best charger. General Robinson is shot through the body, a bad wound. Two of General Sir S. Cotton's officers, his aide-de-camps, who were there as amateurs, suffered. One coming home was shot in the thigh. Many others had narrow escapes, and Lord Wellington remained exposed, untouched! It is really wonderful!

To-day again there was some fighting, but only on our left, a sort of trial of the French strength.

I hear, however, we lost several men, particularly of the 9th. On the whole, with wounded and sick, we shall be much reduced by this week's work, and I still think can scarcely advance safely any further, unless you send men here instead of to Holland ; or unless we can get a good corps of Spaniards to join us under officers who will keep them in order. O'Donnell, the Condé D'Obisbal, is come up again, and will do I think, as he will hang his men until he gets order and obedience. Lord Wellington has also got his full powers renewed by the Spaniards, and may now perhaps try them once more, if tempted to advance after what has happened.

Sunday, 12th December, 3 o'clock.—Every one gone out again, but nothing expected to be done to-day. The French attacked us after sunset last night in force, in hopes, I suppose, of catching us napping again, and getting more baggage ; but it did not succeed. The Germans are kept here to-day. My first letter, up to the 11th, I have sealed and sent, and keep this open in case of more news, for which I must hunt, and then come in and finish this, and after dinner divide my prize maps of this canton, and of the whole seat of the northern war. French maps of this year—great prizes. For the present adieu.

5 *o'clock.*—More fighting again to-day. The French columns appeared, and we threw some shells amongst them. This brought on a quarrel, and we skirmished sharply for a long time ; the Guards concerned principally ; the Adjutant killed, Lieutenant-colonel, and a Captain. I hear of no advantage gained on either side—mere fighting. Our entrenching tools are sent for, so I suppose we are going to make ourselves snug to remain quiet.

6 *o'clock.*—No more news, and no more fighting, but I have just heard that Lieutenant-colonel D—— W—— is shot in the head, and some say killed ; some contradict it altogether. I had told Miss W—— he was well, in a letter just gone to the post. The Paymaster-general and several amateurs got suddenly into fire without intending it the other day. It is better now to stay at home, as one fight is much like any other, and I have now seen some of the best which are likely to happen.

CHAPTER VIII.

FRENCH ATTACK—PLAN OF DESERTION—EXCESSES OF THE
FRENCH—A BASQUE WITNESS—SIR JOHN HOPE—MOVE-
MENTS OF THE ARMY—SALE OF EFFECTS—WELLINGTON'S
SIMPLICITY OF CHARACTER—A FRENCH EMIGRÉ—RETURN
OF SOULT TO BAYONNE.

Head-Quarters, St. Jean de Luz,
December 14, 1813.

MY DEAR M——

As every one is still in the front, and I have
now but a few letters to write on business, I shall
proceed in writing to you, and, if I can, send this by
the delayed packet. Yesterday morning the French
were, I believe, to have been attacked again in our
front, in order to drive them back into Bayonne.
In the morning, however, they were off, and had
disappeared from the disputed ground, and only
appeared in the Bayonne works. This made us
suspect an attack from them on General Hill, who
was on our right, with only some Portuguese, and
his two divisions on the other side of the Nivé.

Reinforcements were ordered accordingly, and all the grandees and amateurs went that way. So it turned out, the French came in large masses and attacked us there, just as we were moving about in our position.

They at first drove the Portuguese brigade there back from a knoll. They rallied, returned, and recovered it. By that time the rest of the two divisions were up ready, and the French came on in more force. The attack became general along the line, and the French were beaten back on all sides with very considerable loss, and without the reinforcements, which were not in time. I know no particulars at all, as Lord Wellington did not return last night to this place, but some who did, say the French were very thick, as they came forward in such masses, and some of their own disheartened prisoners talk of four thousand men and more as their loss. These daily desperate attacks, first on their right and then on their left, and the accounts given by the German Nassau officers, make me suspect very much that Soult will after this be off altogether further to the rear after having obeyed his orders, by a desperate attempt to drive us back into Spain again. I hear that he wrote to Lord Wellington before these five days' fighting, to say that we must positively quit France, and that, to save bloodshed, he wished Lord Wellington would retire of his own accord. I did not learn this, however, from the very best authority.

The day before yesterday I met at dinner the Major of the Nassau regiment, a very pleasant gentleman-like man, aide-de-camp to the Prince, and the very officer who brought the secret verbal order to the Colonel K —— to take the steps he has done. The Major arrived six weeks ago, but they never found the opportunity until now. Similar orders are gone to another battalion with Marshal Suchet, and to a corps of Nassau cavalry there, and we have sent word to our army on that side to try, and let them know that these three battalions have succeeded. The whole was very near failing even this time; he gave us all the particulars.

The French towards evening thought things were not going on quite well, and ordered up all the reserves. Amongst the rest were three battalions, and that of Baden, which lately had been kept much in the rear; when they were all retiring towards their quarters again at dusk, General Villatte (Colonel Downie's old enemy), who commanded the reserve, was obliged to retire to the rear, wounded. He left orders with a stupid old General who succeeded him in command. The Colonel of the Nassau re-

giment was directed by the old man to retire along
the great road. He represented the numbers going
that way and the delay, and proposed a side road.
The old man said, "Well, you will do your best."
The Colonel then thought all would do, and was
about to take his march off, when up came the 34th
regiment, all French, and their commanding officer
said, "*Monsieur Le Colonel, J'ai mes ordres de
vous suivre sur votre route.*" This was most per-
plexing. The Colonel then made an imaginary ob-
stacle at the head of the column, and desired the men
to file one by one slowly. This tired the patience of
the French, who had been out all day. The Colonel
then proposed his plan to the officer commanding
the Baden regiment. He had received no orders,
he said, from his Sovereign, and, after hesitating a
little, declined. Colonel K—— then ordered him
to take another road, and told the French as they
must divide to get home at all, they had better
follow the Baden regiment. The French 34th did
so ; and the others soon began to incline towards
the English, firing away however, but in the air, to
deceive any who might be observing them. They
soon found themselves near enough to send in the
officer first, and the regiment followed in spite of
some shots from our people. The astonishment of
many, who not being in the secret, found them-

selves within the English picket, and fancied they
were all about to be made prisoners, was very considerable : as was their joy when told the true state
of things.

The Major told us they had seen constant service
in Spain, that their Sovereign's contingent for
Spain was about two thousand men, but that the
French kept it up whenever they could to nearly
three thousand, and more at times. He was in
Talavera, and the bugle of one of the battalions
which sounded as they left, and marched through
was English, and I understand was taken from
us at the battle of Talavera. He confessed the
horrors committed in Spain was *" Nous autres"* (as
he was constantly expressing himself), forgetting
he was no longer French, and then correcting himself said, *" par les Français."* He said it was a
practice when the orders were issued to plunder
and burn places which had been deserted by their
inhabitants, to make a great fire near the place so
as to make the inhabitants think a battle was about
to begin, and lead them to retire to some spot near,
out of the way of the fire, but never intending to
desert their homes. The troops then voted it a
deserted town, and begun first to pillage, then to
burn. He described the French army as being
now about fifty-five thousand men, after this

business, of which, however, only about twenty-two, or twenty-three thousands were soldiers, that is veterans, the rest raw recruits and conscripts, of which Bayonne was full, and where you now saw, he said, even the blind and the lame compelled to come forward and serve.

He said they were very ill supplied with everything, and had no forage at all; that one great store of biscuit was spoilt in the church at Bayonne; and that the roads in the rear were so bad that hardly any supplies could arrive but by the river—at least not without the greatest difficulty and labour; that the Dax and Tartas roads were infamous, and the one I went by, Peyrorade and Orthes, very bad. Allowance must be made, I think, in these accounts.

Soult was enraged with the inhabitants for wishing to return home within our lines, and was much provoked at our not having behaved much worse in this country. I have also understood from flag-of-truce officers that the French are excessively angry with their women for all desiring to come here to us. The mayor of Biaritz, I believe, is proclaimed, as having given us assistance, and ordered to be seized as soon as caught. The French were two or three days since in one attack actually in his garden, but could never get into his house.

K 3

Of course he had removed many of his goods, and was on the alert. He has had a picket always in his house and been very liberal. Near that house our guns and the French were within three hundred yards of each other, but neither could get at the opponent on account of the formation of the ground. There was a small wood near, which was a strong point. Lord Wellington, &c., just returned. I must go and pick up news.

Head-Quarters, St. Jean de Luz, December 15th, 1813, Wednesday.—We are now all returned to our civil business again, and I have just been to the Adjutant-general and Lord Wellington, as usual, to congratulate them on their safety, at the same time that I made my reports, and received fresh instructions. I have not time, therefore, to add much to this, which is, I believe, the sixth folio sheet you will receive this mail.

All the reports confirm the account that the French got a severe beating on our right the day before yesterday, and our loss was not that day so severe in comparison with the other affair on our left. Our present position is close round the French and Bayonne, in a semicircle from the sea to the Adour. The advanced posts being from the front of Biaritz and Anglet, on the sea on our left, and so through Arcamgues, Arrauntz, on the Nivé, the centre, where our boat-bridge is, and then through Monguerre, Petit, and Vieux, to La Home, on the Adour, on our extreme right. Some alarm us by a report that head-quarters are to be moved in consequence to Ustaritz, as being on the Nivé, and more centrical, and near the bridges. We all, however, hope otherwise. Some Spaniards are come on now also, and more cavalry are ordered up. Our abode here has quite spoiled us for the wretched places we must crowd into at Ustaritz, down in a muddy hole, with the roads almost impassable around it.

Unless you have a good map, you will find but few of the places I mention, and yet I have omitted two or three in the circle.

[The places were all found in old maps by Robert, a French geographer].

I must go to work to draw charges, so adieu.

I have a most eloquent French, or, rather, Basque witness here, who has been robbed, and whom I am keeping here to give evidence. He pays me daily visits, and acts over the scene in question, and several others, in very high style. The Basques are as proud as our Welsh of their antiquity, and when asked if they are French, say, " *Oh, que non, Basque !*" He tried to insinuate himself into my favour, by reminding me that this

country was once all English, and that the inhabitants had still the memory of that, and favourable feelings accordingly.

Sir John Hope was, including his dress, touched
in seven places, besides a shot in his horse, and
through his large hat. The skin wound, though
slight, is the only wound that gives him pain.
Lord Wellington blames his exposing himself ;
with what face I know not.

Head-Quarters, St. Jean de Luz, December
16*th*, 1813.—Though I have written to you by the
detained mail, which went yesterday, I know you
will expect something by our next, so I begin my
work in time ; as I conclude it will go Sunday as
usual again. I have just heard, the packet which
went from hence the 22nd, with our letters to the
21st November, was found deserted at sea, and
letters, &c., supposed to be taken, or, most likely,
sunk. I think I sent you two long letters by that
packet, with a plan of my house here, and sketch
of it, and the largest proportion of prize Spanish
maps, taken at Vittoria ; begging you to keep
them, and those that come after, safe. It was in
that letter I told you of my narrow escape at St.
Fé from being shot through the head by a dragoon
as I was writing. The ball went between my pen
and my nose, and where my head had been two

seconds before, and one cheek was spattered by the door splinters, and the other by the wall plaster where the ball struck.

We have just got a most alarming report, as far as our comfort is concerned, namely, that we are to move to a little dirty village, called Arrauntz, on the Nivé, worse almost than Frenada, with the exception of one good house, where roads are impassable—almost up to the knees in mud. I believe it certainly was fixed, but Colonel Campbell told me just now he believed the order was deferred; and I am sure I hope so most sincerely, as we are here rather in a state of civilization and comfort.

I dined yesterday at head-quarters, and who should I meet but Count de Gazan's *ci-devant* aide-de-camp, a fine, gentleman-like young man, with whom I dined at Count Gazan's house at that time—Lord Wellington's now. He was then very civil to us. We dined yesterday in his *ci-devant* apartment. He was about to join Marshal Victor in the North, as his aide-de-camp, when I last saw him ; but, being promoted to a chef-de-battalion, this induced him to stop and take the command. It answers to our Lieutenant-colonel ; and he commanded a battalion against General Hill in the last attack. Finding his men running away too fast, he kept in the rear to encourage them, and give them confidence ; stayed there too long, and, in a word, was caught and taken prisoner. He is a tall, stout, good-looking man of twenty-eight, and speaks English well, having been there some time before for education.

I gave him a good breakfast this morning before he set out for Passages, got him a letter to the principal Commissary at Passages, and handed him my father's direction at Somerset House ; desiring him to let him know where he is ultimately quartered in England, and if my father could serve him in any way in London. So be prepared for a letter some time hence from my French acquaintance. He is a staunch Frenchman in everything, but I do not like him the worse for that, or for avowing it openly.

He told me we were not quite so secure in Holland, and that we were not near a peace, but had much yet to do to obtain such a one as we required, for Bonaparte was ambitious and unreasonable, and we were unreasonable also. In some respects I agree, and only hope the Allies will continue moderate. I offered him money, but he said he had lost nothing, and did not require it, and declined any assistance. He said, at the moment he was vexed that our men did not plunder him, as he knew his own people would have done so by us. He seems a shrewd fellow, and was therefore ordered off directly from hence.*

Lord Wellington looks thin, but was in high spirits yesterday. We have more artillery and ammunition passing up to-day to the front, and, I hear, they are making works to strengthen our position, and to be prepared against any other desperate attack. This may be only Lord Wellington's usual prudence, as it does not look like a move on further. Other circumstances, however, do rather look like a movement forwards, and the strengthening this position may be either for the present security, or for a position to retire to in case of accidents, as we have now two rivers in our rear; or, which may be most likely, for both. The fact is, we have above twelve hundred men digging away, and artillery is going up.

My French witness here tells me a friend has just arrived from Bayonne, who informs him, that whilst the movements were going on some days since. Marshal Soult told the leading people of Bayonne, that all who intended to move their valuables to the rear should do so by water immediately, if at all, as circumstances might soon make it impossible for them to do so by water, and the

* He made no application to Mr. Larpent's family, nor did he call at Somerset House.

road would be entirely required by the military in
certain events. This does not look like much
confidence.

Friday, December 17*th, three o'clock, and Sunday, December* 19*th, post-day.*—A report of more
work on the right, and we fancy we have heard much
firing. Lord Wellington is gone off. If things
have not gone on well, or the horses get tired, we
shall have a move yet, I fear very soon, but hope
otherwise most sincerely, that is, if it is only a
move of head-quarters. A forward movement of
the army will be otherwise, as it will prove to me
Lord Wellington thinks something is to be done
by it. Our cavalry is moving up fast · this looks
like a movement. It spreads out by Cambo on
our right. I am also assured by a French officer
here in our service in the Quarter Master-general's
department, that the French cavalry are fast filing
to the rear, and have already passed Mont de
Marsan, my former abode, and that many of the
old soldiers are from necessity sent back to Bordeaux to compel some refractory conscripts there
to move, as they are a little wilful. He also told
me the loss of the French (desertion included), in
the late affairs last week, was, in the whole, about
thirteen thousand men. He is however a sanguine
man, remember that. We are also said to have

taken two or three boats on the Adour, above
Bordeaux.

*Head-Quarters, St. Jean de Luz, five o'clock,
Sunday, December* 19*th,* 1813.   I have nothing to
add, so shall seal up.   I am just come from the
seaside, where we can now scarcely stand for the
wind, and are, on the high walk, quite wet with
the spray.   A violent gale of some hours has
caused this, and I have been watching a vessel
off here for a long time which has been in considerable danger, but is at last safe in Saçoa harbour.   She was most uneasy at sea, made signals of
distress, and the pilot boats ventured out, and by
their help and working hard with the capstan on
an anchor carried out, she has at last worked her
way in.

I met yesterday at dinner Colonel Barnard,
who was lately shot through the body.   Colonel
Rooke is dead.   I feared it must be so, from
what I heard yesterday.   He could not eat
anything, grew rapidly weaker, and the suppu-
ration formed a mass clear through his body
from one orifice of the wound to the other,
and not properly round the ball so as to assist
its extraction.   Lieutenant-colonel West is well:
I saw him to-day, not touched.   The report of
his being killed arose from his having sent a

horse to the rear—I believe to walk. At Captain
Watson's sale yesterday (he is dead, and was of the
Guards), I bought a very tolerable saddle, with
holsters, about half worn, for eighteen dollars, which
is here considered cheap. I bid 15s. for a curry-
comb and brush, bad, but of English make, and
in England worth about 3s. or 4s. : it went for a
guinea? I also bid for a Suffolk punch horse up
to two hundred dollars, but Major Daring outbid
me, though it was certainly very dear.

A party of Bayonne sailors have just arrived here
I am told, who have come over to us. Bayonne
envies this place now. If we stay, and have money,
things will come in here soon from the French, for
the geese they bring in sell for four dollars instead
of 4s. as before we came, and so with other things ;
we have also got some good French cattle to eat.

*Head-Quarters, St. Jean de Luz, December
21st, 1813.*—Our furious stormy weather continues, and almost continual rain, attended yesterday by a most violent clap of thunder ; such
repeated gusts of wind I scarcely ever witnessed.
The inhabitants say, it will last as long as we have
the wind from the sea. At the same time it is
not at all cold, and I have no fire except when I
have been caught in the wet, and am very damp.
This happens if you stir for five hundred yards, as

the rain comes with a gust in a few seconds. The thermometer in my room, without a fire, has been constantly almost above temperate, and at times above sixty. We are at present all quiet again here, and invitations are flying about for Christmas dinners on Saturday next.

Marshal Soult is angry with the inhabitants for being friends with us. He is now circulating proclamations on our right, exhorting the people to form Guerilla corps and to turn brigands. If we continue to behave well, I do not think he will easily persuade them to do this. The Spaniards who demand rations and contributions, &c., against orders, and are not so orderly as they might be, (the few that are in France, that is,) may perhaps provoke them to arms, but I hope not. We now go about the roads here as safe as in Spain; the only marauders indeed are the followers of our own army and runaway Spaniards and muleteers. Our own army is behaving particularly well, and now give me a little leisure occasionally, which, whenever the weather permits, I employ in exercise.

To my great joy to-day, and still more, I suspect, to that of my horses, I have got a good truss of English hay—140 lbs. weight. This is a treasure. But to balance good and evil, the Commissary has given us no corn during the last three days, So we go on ! Many of the cavalry horses get neither, so we must submit.

In spite of the rough weather, we yesterday got a packet and English mail, and I received a letter from you of the 6th and 7th December, and papers from the 4th to the 7th. You confirm our accounts of the loss of the mail of the 21st November, and of two letters of mine to you. I only hope they are sunk, though I recollect nothing particular in them.

———

I have no doubt —— plays the great man very well, and puts on all the dignity of a Jack in office. He likes the thing, and has a turn for humbug, of which there is so much all over the world in every line, and which is often of such infinite use to those who can adopt it. I think it very tiresome, and only rejoice that it is not the fashion here at head-quarters. From Lord Wellington downwards, there mighty little. Every one works hard, and does his business. The substance and not the form is attended to : in dress, and many other respects, I think almost too little so. The maxim, however, of our Chief, is, " Let every one do his duty well, and never let me hear of any difficulties about any-thing :" and that is all he cares about. I suppose one should fall by degrees into a love of representation, and keeping one's self up in the world, as it is called (by those who have not much else to float them), by habit and practice ; but I must say, as yet I continue to think it far best to be able to do what you please, as you please, and when you please, and that provided nothing is ever done that in the least approaches to a shabby or ungentleman-like action, so that the opinion of those whose opinion is worth having is secured. The sort of incense that is often obtained from the silly majority through exterior humbug is not worth the price at which it is purchased. My vanity takes a different turn, and I pique myself upon other things.

I attended another sale yesterday of Colonel Martyn's effects. It was quite ridiculous how some old things sold, Two second-hand nightcaps, costing about 1s. 6d. each, new, in England, fetched 13s. This results partly from distress, partly from fun in the bidders. Old towels 5s. each ; blankets 25s. I always feel hurt at seeing all an officer's stock sold in this way, even to his ragged shirts and stockings, tooth brushes, &c. ; everything ransacked. It was very near being my case, also, when I was taken prisoner. Mr. Jesse's stock was sold, and he is not a little distressed in consequence. How much more so should I have been you may well guess. I have received a note from Lieutenant-colonel E—— to dine with him on Christmas-day, and have accepted, though I suspect I shall lose a great party at Lord Wellington's by so doing, as he generally asks heads of departments on those days. I own, however, that I prefer his smaller parties, when fewer grandees are there, and Lord Wellington talks more and we drink less. A great party is almost always stupid, unless there is good singing or good speechifying ; and I have now seen all the lions likely to be there. By-the-bye, our Spanish lions carry their heads wonderfully erect now, and are prouder than any peacocks ; or rather, I might say, they are now true Spaniards.

Yesterday I dined at Lord Wellington's, and had another adventure. I recognized an emigré friend at Mont de Marsan, of whom I had been, during my stay there, very shy, fearful lest a malicious report should get about that I was intriguing with the royalists. I reminded him of his questions, &c., and speaking to me several times, and I now explained myself and conduct. He was much surprised at seeing me in my red coat, but immediately recollected me, and said I had given him then all the information he wanted. My answers were short, but all true certainly. He has brought some congratulations to the Comte de Grammont

from the persons now on his *ci-devant* estates, and
their wishes for old times and old landlords. He
had got some money here, and is, I suppose to go
to work somehow for the good cause. He is very
sanguine; but though I like and respect the
emigrés, I always mistrust their view of things.

A foolish Portuguese, whom I got sentenced to
be shot, escaped three days ago, and was off; but
like a fool, he boasted in Spain of his performances,
was in consequence re-taken, and to-day is to be
hung.

December 26th, Post-day.—Another of my
French friends came in from Bayonne yesterday,
—the principal banker at Bayonne, who gave me
money for my bill, and was so friendly to us all,
and to me in particular, and for whom I loaded
my pockets so quietly with so many letters—above
a hundred in number. He has ostensibly come
to receive the 110*l.* still due to him from five of
our officers, and which Lord Wellington intended
to send him on my representation : but he has also
obtained leave from Soult to supply us with claret,
&c., and is partly come about that. The French,
I conclude, are compelled to try this method of
making a little money; and the Marshal Soult
being, I have no doubt, ill-paid, will go halves in
the profit. I suspect my friend, however, may have

further views also, as he is a Spanish and English merchant as well as banker, and of course a decided enemy to Berlin and burning decrees, and to war in general, which is now nearly synonymous with being an enemy to Bonaparte. Lord Wellington sent him to the Commissary-general to talk matters over.

We have been all quiet here this week, except a little cavalry skirmish on our right. The French cavalry, as I hear, had driven in some of Don Murillo's Spaniards, with Hill in that quarter, and two sqadrons of our 18th Hussars were ordered to drive the French back. They did this, as ordered, without loss, but, as usual, would do more, and pushing hastily on, fell in with the French infantry support, which is generally near at hand to the cavalry advance, got a volley or two, and lost a Captain and several men in consequence.

Our people will suppose that the French lurk about the country without system or order as they do, whereas, however cowed and beaten they may be, the system and order and habitual rules remain.

Some more of Don Carlos d'Espagne's troops filed up from Irun yesterday, and turning off about a mile short of this, went through Ascian towards our right—about five thousand in the whole.

Murillo's people are several of them put under arrest by Lord Wellington for misconduct. They complain that the men get sick in consequence, to which he replies, "Then behave better, and that will not be the case."

Some of our artillery-men have by accident burnt one of the best of the few remaining houses at St. Sebastian, worth twenty thousand dollars as the Spaniards say, and about to be let for six hundred dollars a-year. This will be quite convincing to the Conciso at Cadiz, and perhaps to the regency, that we burnt the town on purpose, and are now finishing our job. It is unlucky to give this handle to these most unconquerably jealous Spaniards, and already the engineers and few English at St. Sebastian's are most unpopular. Our weather is now much improved, and turned to frost for the first time this month, which improves our roads, our spirits, and our prospects: the sea, however, has been for these two last days tremendous, and washed over our stone bulwark where we walk, and has cut off our supply of corn these three days from Passages. I was yesterday caught there when walking with General Pakenham and General Murray: the Quarter-Master-general ran one way, the Adjutant-general and I another; the former escaped, and so did the latter and I, though the foam and surf

burst upright, close to us, above our heads, and
then washed our legs midway up ; but the force
was broken, and we were not moved, only wetted.
The natives and many of our officers think this
roaring ocean predicts more bad weather here again,
but I hope it only proves a storm some two hundred
miles off in the main ocean, as I have always
observed there is little connection here between
our land-storms and the state of the sea, which
seems to be moved by other causes, of which I think
one is the agitation caused by the flood spring-
tides.

Monday.—Marshal Soult is returned again to
Bayonne. Lord Wellington, &c., are all out with
the hounds.

CHAPTER IX.

REPORTS FROM FRANCE—MORE DESERTION—ANECDOTE OF
GENERAL STEWART—WELLINGTON AND HIS CASUALTY RE-
TURNS—THE COURTESIES OF WAR—SCARCITY OF TRANSPORTS
—WELLINGTON AND THE TRIAL-PAPERS - SIR G. COLLIER.

Head Quarters, St. Jean de Luz.
January 1, 1814.

MY DEAR M——

IN the first place, many happy new years
to you and all your party! And when this is
said, I have almost said all, as we are now quite
quiet here, and have no news from you, and have
no events of our own to communicate. Reports of
an English mail we have repeatedly received, but
it never arrives in fact; and we almost fancy that
one of the packets coming from you must have
been lost, as well as the one going from hence. It
may, however, arise from our having had three of
the vessels at once on this side of the water.

You will be surprised when I tell you I had an
old French woman, and a young Spanish one to

L 2

breakfast with me this morning, on their way through to Bayonne, from Bilboa. I had made arrangements for six mules, and an ox-car, to carry their baggage, &c., but they mistook the tide in their directions, and the baggage is only now arrived this moment, so they cannot go until to-morrow. They are the wife and mother of a Monsieur Dabedrille, at Bayonne, *ci-devant* principal *Directeur de l'Octroi de Bilboa*, who fled so quickly after the Vittoria business, that he left all his baggage and females behind him. He was very civil to Colonel Fitzgerald, who had under-taken to get him his wife restored, and as the Colonel was not exchanged, I undertook it, got Lord Wellington's leave, and here they are, so far on their way safe. Not having just now much business, I have had time to attend a little to these good ladies, and they are really very pleasant and well bred, but just now very dirty, having been six days on board a Spanish coaster (of Bilboa), to get here.

We have just now got beautiful weather, clear, frosty mornings— that is white frost, and the ground just crisp, a little fog early, and a cool breeze from the Pyrenees, from the south-east, and a bright sun during the day.

The only news we have here is a report of the

defeat of Davoust, through the French, and an account which General Wimpfen has just given me of the Austrians having taken possession of Switzerland. The French here are hard at work, drilling conscripts, who arrive in considerable numbers, and turning up the ground, as usual, in all directions. I suppose we shall also, as usual, wait until they have nearly done their job, and by that time, when the ground is dry, turn them out of their laborious defences. It is quite extraordinary how all their former position was covered with the effects of their labour.

The inhabitants continue to come in here to us every day, and now, by degrees, we get cattle, &c. from them. Desertion from the French has also been common, five or six men in a day, and many French, not Germans, young lads, sick of their work. I now hear the Swiss have declared against France; that is a step more gained, if true. An officer, who was prisoner at Bayonne, on the 13th, the day of General Hill's affair on the right, says the French were most sanguine that morning at Bayonne; they said two of our divisions were caught in a trap, and that they would, General and all, be prisoners. They were quite in spirits, but towards evening, when the officer inquired where our General was, he could get no one to answer him, or talk on the subject. All were sulky.

Report says also that Soult is gone again, and farther back, some say sent for to Paris. These are curious times, in short, upon the whole.

One of our hay vessels, to plague us, has got into Bayonne, and the French officers at the outposts taunt us, by saying, that they find English hay very good. It is very provoking as we have now nothing again, in consequence, to give our animals.

Sunday, Post-day.—I understand there is no packet as yet at Passages, to go with the letters. I have, after three hours' bother, packed off my party this morning; four great trunks, two old women, and one young one, in an ox-car; and four more large trunks, and a quantity of bedding, and et ceteras of all kinds, on four mules, and one lady, and a man-servant, on horseback. My old French woman, now she is safe out of Spain, does nothing but abuse the Spaniards, their language, their manners, their country, &c., and above all, their stupidity in society.

I must now return to the work of drawing charges, as I have business to prepare immediately. I hope there is not another job now passing my window, as there is an uproar, and

seven Spanish prisoners going along bound to the
Provost guard.

We have now established a sort of little telegraph
of signals to the right and in front, to let Lord Wellington know immediately if anything is going
forward.

P.S.—I think I never told you a little anecdote
of our General Stewart, who is brave, and always
gets his aide-de-camp, &c., into some bad blows,
in consequence, if he does not get one himself.
His people about him on the 13th were all
touched, and he was nearly alone. An officer of
the name of Egerton came up, and whilst there a
shell burst between them; Stewart said, " A shell,
sir! very animating!" and then kept Egerton
there talking on.

Head-Quarters, St. Jean de Luz, January 4th,
1814.—Here we are still without any news from
your side of the water, and of course, most anxious.
On this side we seem, however, to be preparing
something for you to talk about; at least, appearances look like another affair. The day before
yesterday (Sunday) all was quiet, and on Monday
(yesterday) Lord Wellington ordered out his
hounds, and went off early himself. In the middle
of the day, however, the signal was made that the
French were in motion; Lord March and Gordon

went off to Lord Wellington, and he did not return last night. To-day the troops have all been on the alert, as the French are said to be still moving on our right, and in fact, rather on our rear. The Guards were off early from hence to replace the light division, who went to the right, and all seems moving in that direction. No firing has, however, been heard, and I understand nothing has been done to-day. I went as far as Guethary, and up to the church tower, from whence the view is very extensive, but saw nothing in particular. The last report was, that the French still advanced on our right. If they persist in this, I think we must have a fight, and a sharp one, probably, on that side to-morrow, but as the staff are all out, I know nothing certain.

Two or three days since we took a little island in the Adour, almost without loss, which will enable us to molest the navigation more effectually than we do, though already it is rather impeded, even at night, and almost totally by day. A contest about the island was rather expected, but not this bold move of the French in our rear. If they persist and fail, I think with the two Gaves in their rear, we may, perhaps, make them suffer severely for their enterprize. Marshal Soult's supposed absence looks now rather like a *ruse de guerre*.

We have Spaniards on our right, and in the valley of Bastan, who perhaps may now come in again for a little fighting, and I hope they may, for if the French work constantly on the British and Portuguese, and you continue to send men to Holland, we shall by degrees get too weak for our situation.

Lord Wellington at dinner on Sunday directed some jokes at Major D——, who makes out the returns, because he wanted to make a grand total of wounded, &c., after the late five days' fighting. He laughed, and said, all might go wrong from this innovation, but he was determined he would have no more grand totals until he got another Vittoria without more loss; that the loss was always great enough, in all conscience, without displaying it in this ostentatious manner, and that he would not have every drummer and every officer, &c., killed or wounded in the five days, all added up in one grand total, but that at least the croakers should have the trouble themselves of adding up all the different losses, and making it out for themselves.

The weather is just now delightful, and we have had as yet nothing which can properly be called winter. During the last ten days the sea has been

L 3

quite smooth, and we have not even had a white
frost. The people say they think the first bad
season is over now, and we shall not have much
more bad weather until near March : I only hope
this will prove correct.

A French carriage and a car were waiting at the
French outposts to receive my ladies, and they all
got in safe. This was managed by sending in a
message the day before. A certain communication
with Bayonne is also now open, for yesterday we
had an arrival of French watches, rings, trinkets,
and silk dresses. We carry on war in a very civilized manner, especially if a little anecdote I heard
yesterday be correct. I was told that one of our
officers, I believe Major Q——, was riding a troublesome horse close to the French pickets, and
partly from the violence of his horse, and partly
from his own inadvertence, he got close to a French
sentinel. The latter called out several times that
he was French, and ordered him off, and at last
presented his bayonet. The horse still plunging
on, and the officer apparently not understanding
the man, the French sentry turned the horse the
other way by the bridle, and sent him back without
offering any harm to either beast or rider, though
he might have killed or taken both.

This morning we had another instance on our side. A French officer's wife came in from Bayonne to follow her husband, a prisoner in England. We had a boat in from Sacoa to take her upon the beach, to carry her round by sea to Passages, and an order from Lord Wellington waiting for her there, for a passage to England as expeditiously as circumstances would permit.

Wednesday, 5th January.—No one came back last night, and St. Jean de Luz is almost deserted; scarcely a red coat to be seen. The ladies are in some alarm, and only some inquiring doctors and commissaries are to be seen about the streets. I have in the mean time such an accumulation of business for Lord Wellington that I shall be almost fearful of seeing him—five Courts-martial, one of about ninety pages, another eighty. He always complains, and yet I think he likes to read these cases, and know himself exactly all that is going on. I have just been out to pick up news, but in vain, and I am sorry to say I have been driven back by a slight shower; I hope, however, it is no more, and not a preface to another batch of rainy weather. Money has been so short here that I could only tempt them to give me some doubloons immediately by accepting a part of my pay on England in another Treasury Bill.

Friday, January 7th.—Lord Wellington is not yet returned here, we are, therefore, still deserted, but nothing has been done. The French have been manœuvring for these three days on our right flank, but in vain, as our General was ready for them. Yesterday, however, he was nearly bringing them to blows. A part of their force remained on our side of the Adour, between the Nivé and the Bidocke. This was too near our position, and they were to have been driven across, but prudently went away in good time of their own accord, consequently nothing was done, and I think nothing will be done just now.

The French head-quarters here are at (I believe) Peyrehorade, a town on the Gave, which I have passed through, of some little river commerce. In our present suspense we have at last been amused, yesterday, by the arrival of two mails, and I have got letters, papers, &c.

You kill men for me faster than I do in reality, and that is enough. I am only aware of forty-one having been shot or hung since I have been in the country; and that is quite enough, too, you will say, almost as many as you hang in all England in a year. You were quite right about the lost letter from me; it contained a full description of St. Jean de Luz, and of my horrible muddy journey from

St. Fé to this civilized place, with a sketch of my house and its vicinity, &c., a ground plot of my quarter, which, if I have time and room, I will repeat. And as you do not congratulate me on my escape from being shot, I suppose that story was there also.

Later.—As Lord Wellington is still away, I continue to scribble to you, snatching a little time from my newspapers for the purpose. You ask about this place. It has been a very flourishing town, and of considerable trade, but is much in decay; this partly before the late wars, from the bar having increased, so that only small vessels can get in now, and the evil increases still. At low water the river only ripples over the bar of sand, scarcely a foot deep, and at times the river is choked up by the sand, so that it cannot make its way out, and floods the town. This happened twice last year, but has not been the case this, though at times the bed of the river has been quite changed, and the water nearly stopped.

Sacoa is a very safe harbour; for small vessels drawing under ten feet, quite safe. They lie there high and dry, according to the tide. The houses of the former merchants are rather magnificent though some are in ruins, and their number, for the size of the town, considerable. It has been called a sort of little Paris for the Basques. Near the sea the water has been, and is, gaining on the town and bay. There are many ruins; one is part of an old convent, now beyond the sea-wall, and almost in the sea, and some say a whole street has been washed away. The great sea-wall made by Bonaparte, six hundred yards long, is to save the town, and makes a good dry walk.

Sibour is also a very large village, or small town, of inferior houses, where two brigades of Guards are, and two other regiments of Lord Aylmer's brigade, besides some staff cavalry, &c. Most of the better houses have French papers up from Paris, and it looks very well. The whole wall forms one landscape, like tapestry—sea-ports from Vernet or Claude, &c.; some in colours, some in bistre or an imitation of Indian ink, some Chinese, but in better perspective. The brown and black are very pretty. Most of the walls are papered. The lower parts of the houses are all a sort of warehouse (where they are not shops); this serves us for stabling, but they are flagged, which having no straw is noisy, and they smell much also. Almost all the men of a better sort went away from St. Jean de Luz; several women stayed, mostly old, and many have since returned; but no society or anything of that sort is as yet set on foot here. The deputy mayor, who stayed, sold all the wine he could appropriate, his own, and all unclaimed, as well as other things, and is making money of us very fast, I believe. The town is now all a market or fair, and full of Spaniards and Portuguese, as well as French and Bascos, all pillaging poor John Bull, by selling turkeys for 25s. and 30s., and fowls for 12s. and 14s.

The people from Bilboa have been most active. Little has arrived from England or Lisbon as yet, which I wonder at, but the danger of the coast is, I presume, the cause. During our bad weather ten vessels of ours found their way into Bayonne, one with fifty-two Irish bullocks, by which we lost part of the best beef we ever get, and one with seven hundred trusses of hay, others with biscuit, &c. This is very provoking. The Bayonne mayor showed us the post list of the whole taken in each ship. How we shall get on with our animals I know not, as I am told they hear from England, in the Commissariat, there is but little hay on the sea for us, from want of transport, and there is no straw at all now within thirteen leagues, or about forty miles, from hence to be got. I am, however, advised to send for it, and if I find this movement comes to nothing I shall do so to-morrow.

It is fortunate we are so near the sea, and have
some advantage as to transport in the river Nivelle,
also, as our transport is much diminished by desertion of the muleteers from want of pay. The
army is more numerous than when at Frenada
and in Portugal, and our transport is now less.
Were we to wander into France (as you suppose),
away from the coast, we should find it difficult to
live at all. The boats of this place are famous.
and the men stayed here, or have escaped here,
and are all in our pay now, and thus things are
brought round from Passages here by sea, and
then up to the division by the river as far as
Ustaritz, where they are then distributed to the
mules of each division. Even with this help the
army cannot be supplied with rum, except by
buying it on the spot, very dear, of the suttlers, as
all our remaining mules nearly are required for
bread and a little corn for the staff. The meat
supplies itself in a way—that is, about two-thirds
only of the flesh which leaves Palencia, &c., in
Spain, arriving here, falls under the butcher's
knife, besides the number which die on the road ;
and yet all that can be stopped, when fagged or
lame, are distributed at the stations on the way.
The suttlers, by the great profit they make, can
pay the muleteers as high as two dollars a day for

each mule to carry up their produce, making us pay for it in the end. This evil increases, for our muleteers, who only have one dollar a day for each mule (and enough in all conscience), are tempted to desert and get into the service of the suttlers, who thus supply the men with rum only at a dear rate, when we cannot do it. Our muleteers are now owed twenty-one months' pay for each mule ; they have, therefore, their own way, and are under no control at all. Nothing but a sort of *esprit de corps*, and the fear of losing all claim to the debt, makes them keep with us at all, and we must submit to their fraud and carelessness, and have no remedy.

As an instance, I may mention that one brigade of mules, who had twenty-four thousand pounds of barley given to them to bring here, five leagues from Passages, only delivered eighteen thousand, and openly, almost, admitted, they had taken the rest, which I suppose they had sold to raise money. We could only set off the value against their debt, for fear of losing them without getting others. There was a grand consultation the other day ; present, Lord Wellington, the Commissary-general and his people, General Alava the Spanish General, and most of the principal Spanish Capistras or directors of the mules and owners, to settle what could be done. They resolved to make the arrears all a debt, to acknowledge it, and then begin a sort of new score. This is in imitation of the Portuguese; only they do not pay the debt at all, but wipe off the arrears. One month's pay was also given by bills on the Treasury at a great discount, but this was something to go on with, and we have not Marshal Beresford's absolute power to control these Spaniards, as he does the Portuguese. Somehow, however, you see we get on.

Head-Quarters, St. Jean de Luz, Sunday, January 9th, post-day again.—As to length at least, you shall have no reason to complain this mail, though I am set to work again at business; for on Friday night all our warriors returned home to their respective quarters, and the Commander-in-Chief to his papers. The latter had so increased upon him in his five days' absence, that he was quite overwhelmed; and when I went in with a great bundle to add to them, he put his hands before his eyes and said, "Put them on that table; and do not say anything about them now, or let me look at them at all."

This week's manœuvring has this time not ended in smoke, but without smoke, as nearly as possible, for our men could not get within a long shot of the French, without following them beyond what our present plans would admit. They remained a short time on our side the river Arrun, as it is called, in Casini's great map, and Gambouri, in my part of the French National Atlas, a small river which runs by La Bastide and falls into the Adour, near Urt, a place half-way between Bayonne and where the Gaves fall into the Adour.

We collected on the heights above Bastide, and made the signal by a little mountain gun to advance. The French made use of the same signal to commence their retreat across the river, and scarcely a shot was fired. La Bastide, which is on this side of the river, we never entered; but remaining satisfied with that line, the matter ended there; and a change of weather, to rain of no trifling kind, will, I think, oblige both parties to be quiet for some little time again, until sun and air return to us without wet, and dry roads enable the troops to move a little in this difficult country. It is at present very hard work to get on, even in the best roads, and across the country, which is much intersected with streams and rivers, and has only clayey poached up roads, and strong fences of hedge and ditch; it is almost impassable. Lord Wellington, I believe, always went back to his brother Marshal, Beresford, at Ustaritz, to which place he sent for some English hay for his horses. The Adjutant-general's department remained mostly at Hasparen, which is, I understand a very pretty small town in a rich cultivated valley of meadows, where they fell in with a small stock of excellent hay, not quite eaten by our cavalry, who are in that part of the country.

All the head-quarters' people have come back safe and sound; but with horses a little knocked up, and rather stiff with riding about twelve or even fourteen hours a-day. Most of them, however, I think look the better for the exercise. The most fagged of all I saw was our naval hero, Sir G. Collier, with his lame leg. He had ridden everywhere after Lord Wellington in hopes of seeing a fight, and coming in, I suppose, for another knock on shore, but all in vain. He says, the French never will stand when he comes, and nothing is ever done. He is about to leave this station.

And now for a little account of our Spaniards, to show you how they plague Lord Wellington. We have undertaken to assist and direct, with our engineers, the putting of St. Sebastian a little into order, and into a state of defence. The actual working party are, however, nearly all Spanish;

the latter have nearly all deserted, and little or nothing is going on but quarrels between our people and the Spaniards in authority, who thwart them. At first Lord Wellington thought we were to blame, and seemed angry; but he told Col. E—— at last, " If they go on so, d—— them, they may finish the job for themselves ; but go over and see about it, and make a report to me."

Later.—Another English mail arrived, and I have now another letter from you of the 27th and 28th, papers to the 27th, &c. The great news yours contained as to Lord Castlereagh we had heard through the French outposts five days since, only stating that he had actually landed at Morlaix, on his way to Manheim, to the general congress, for a peace. This was believed before your account came, as it agreed with the general tenor of the late English news ; at least I thought so, for one. Whether it will end in a peace, however, I think very doubtful, especially if Bonaparte finds that in consequence of this negociation he keeps all quiet in France, and the conscription, &c., goes on without resistance, and his armies in March next are formidable. If he can once assume an imposing position, I doubt whether he will come into the terms of the Allies. *Mais c'est à voir*, and he has much to do to put himself in such a position.

Many of his conscripts here join almost without any uniforms or necessaries for a soldier, yet every deserter who comes in has everything nearly new, and is better provided for than any of ours, except the few who have just had their new clothing, &c., of which the Guards, who, by the bye, returned here last night to their old quarters, form part. Just now the Italians begin to desert the French, and say it is in consequence of their having heard that their division, which was marched to the rear some short time since, was all disarmed and treated as prisoners of war　This may not be fact ; but the effect is that many Italians come over to us.

CHAPTER X.

RUMOURS OF WAR—THE RIVAL DINNER TABLES—" SLENDER BILLY "—BONAPARTE'S TRICKERY—SPANISH VIOLENCE—WELLINGTON WITH THE HOUNDS—FRENCH AND ENGLISH ASPECTS ; THE OUTSIDES OF THE NATIONS.

Head Quarters, St. Jean de Luz,
January 11, 1814.

MY DEAR M——

THOUGH I do not feel the inspiration of a Quaker to make this promise well, but rather just now the plain duty of one of the establishment, yet, having leisure, I begin my weekly task. Fine weather is now returned, and I have no doubt before we have been quiet another week, if this lasts, we shall be stirred up a little by the French. At present, all our usual avocations are proceeding, and all is quiet.

The only event in my own establishment is the having taken a Spanish lad at present, in addition to my other servants, but it will end in an exchange from an idle Portuguese, who does nothing. I found the lad begging, and in misery, by the sea-side, and asked his history. He told me he was without father and mother, and from a village two leagues beyond Madrid ; that he had been under-stable servant to a French Commandant, who had gone wounded from Bayonne to the rear, towards Paris, and had turned him off. He therefore came back here, towards Spain. I at first only gave him food, and then, that I might not have to try him, took him to General Alava, who promised to send him to General Frere, to make a drummer of him. The next morning he called upon me before he started, and as I rather fancied his looks, I have taken him on trial, and he seems active and useful. I only hope he will not return my charity by rob-bing me, of which there is some risk.

A party of our suttling merchants here behaved ill the other night, by insulting a sick officer ; the worst among them escaped. One is now in confine-ment, and I have sent in his charge. They are all in a terrible fright of military law. I believe he will not be tried if he makes an apology; but it has answered Lord Wellington's intention, in con-vincing these men that there is law here, and that they are followers of the army, and liable to that law.

On the neutral ground, on the great road to

Bayonne, between our pickets and the French, in front of Biaretz, there are, at present, in one of the houses unoccupied by either party, three young damsels alone there. They are rather pretty and interesting, and all say very modest. For a time General Stopford, I believe, out of gallantry, put a safeguard there, but I understand it was considered out of our position, and there was some quizzing. So the damsels are left quiet and alone again. They come daily into our lines, to bring milk, &c., and some flirtation goes on ; but there they are safe. This is creditable to both sides.

I am told that the people at Hasparem, when the French approached the place last week, and it was thought might occupy it, were manifestly alarmed and dissatisfied, and wished us to stay. This might be from the fear of a conflict there, or from the benefits now derived from us, when the first irruption and mischief are over. Fowls are still, near there, to be had for 2s. each ; and turkeys from 7s. or 9s. ; but this will not last, as people here have given, and others now ask, as much as 12s. for fowls, and 30s. for turkeys—even more. General Cole, as we advanced, bought nine geese, at a dollar each ; and this was grand pay, and not from fear. Here they are 25s. each. The former was about the price when I was here before.

Later.—How uncertain everything is with us! Marshal Beresford's aide-de-camp is just come in to Lord Wellington, and there is some stir on our right again. Lord Wellington, and several others, are off that way, and I am told the former stays out all night : this looks as if something was suspected. I dine to-day at head-quarters, and am to go as usual, though he is out. He asked me yesterday, but I told him General Hill had asked me three days before, and expected me. " Very well," said he, " but I advise you to come to me, nevertheless, as you will get a much better dinner ; for General Hill gives the worst dinners going." To General Hill's, however, I went ; and though plain fare, compared to Lord Wellington's, whose table is just now very good, and extremely improved, I got what I call a very good dinner.

If any dependence could be placed on appearances, I should say nothing important was agitating to-day ; for I saw Lord Wellington after he had seen the aide-de-camp, and he read a long letter quietly through, and seemed quite at his ease ; but he takes all that arises so coolly that this proves nothing. A sudden change again to rain will, I think, damp the plans of the French, if they had any, as well as give all those gone off to the right a miserable ride, as it seems well set in for the day. Wind and wet seem here to be winter.

What a change has arisen for our young Prince of Orange, who was here! I only hope he will not be spoilt by success and prosperity. In a little time, after all, I should not be surprised at his looking back at the time he spent here at head-quarters as the pleasantest part of his life. Slender Billy was his nick-name with those who were in timate with him, and he knew it; for one day, at dinner, Lord Fitzroy Somerset, not knowing he was present, said, "Where is Slender Billy to-day?" Upon which the Prince put his head forward, and called out, " Here I am, Fitzroy : what do you want ?"

January 12*th*.—Lord Wellington and his party came back to dinner yesterday. The cause of the bustle was as follows. We had in our possession a mill which belonged rather to the French position than to ours; they attacked it, and, after some brisk firing, it was abandoned to them, and then all was quiet again. This news passed Lord Wellington on the road, but missed him, or he would not have gone on so far as he did. Ustaritz is about fifteen good miles from hence, and the road in parts almost up to a horse's belly. Lord Wellington rode there in the rain in two hours and ten minutes, and back in two hours and a half, up and down hills and through the clay : this proves a horse.

The next piece of news you will, probably, hear first ; but if you should not, you have to learn that the cunning Bonaparte has been making a treaty with King Fernando VII. privately, about a peace with Spain, and that he has sent it to the Cortes for their approval, and has appointed an ambassador for that purpose to Madrid. The gubernador, or preceptor and major domo of King Ferdinand, is either at Madrid, or on his way thither. Spain, and Madrid in particular, is said to be in much agitation. The Cortes are to meet the 15th of January. This is a very artful plan to create jealousies between us, if not to procure a partial peace. We shall see now of what the Regency and Cortes are made. They have in professions bullied much, and resolved never to treat at all whilst a Frenchman remained in Spain. How they will act up to their resolution is to be seen.

Friday, January 14th.—We have now French papers up to the 3rd from Paris, and have got Bonaparte's valedictory address, on setting out for the army in France, to fight on old French territory. This, I think, if the Allies persist, must end the business soon, for if he is well beaten, there must certainly be a rising in France ; and if he beats the Allies, we shall, in my opinion, have a peace, except that he seems determined, even now, not to give up Holland, and that we must at all events retain, if possible. The crisis is, however, apparently approaching, and that rapidly.

We remain here *in statu quo.* French desertion is diminishing, and seems for the moment quiet. Our only event has been the folly of two Portuguese officers near the Adour. They had had a long parley with the French, were, I believe, drinking together, but somehow were persuaded by their French new acquaintance to pass over the river for a dance, or wine, or some reason of that sort, under a promise of being allowed to return safe. They went, however, and have never got back. Lord Wellington has written to Gazan, reminding him of his having sent back six French soldiers, who were taken by the Portuguese in the heat of the campaign, owing to a similar promise or understanding, not having been known to them as made to the French. Lord Wellington claims the two Portuguese in the same way as taken by a breach of faith in the French officers. If this is not acceded to, he then requests that the two officers may be put for some time into close confinement or arrest, which, he says, they deserve, and might probably meet here if restored. As yet no answer is arrived.

A French dragoon of the 21st chasseurs, a deserter, came in yesterday, giving a curious account of his reason for deserting. He says he had been fourteen years in the French service, and was now a corporal; that his own Captain's nephew had lately joined as a private in his troop, that he, the corporal, had to place this man on duty, that he was not tractable or obedient, and that he was obliged to strike him with the flat of his sword; that the nephew told the uncle, and, when they returned, the Captain, as soon as he met the deserter, gave him a severe blow on the face with his fist, and that, in consequence, he immediately got on his horse, and came off to us. He is a fine-looking soldier; and, though he has sold his horse for a hundred dollars, says, he now repents much what he was, in the heat of the moment, induced to do; but it is now too late, the deed is done, and he must persevere.

I forgot to tell you, in my last, of an act of Spanish violence at Vittoria, which has caused a strong sensation in the English army, especially at Vittoria. The Honourable Captain G——, of the 94th, was quartered there, and had had some intrigue with a girl. He at first took her home to his quarter. Her friends had recourse to the police. The armed police came, and were in the house, to take the girl; Captain G—— resisted, and the police were fairly turned out again by him and his servant. When out of the house, they are said to have formed, as it were, and then to have fired in through the door in cool blood, and with no particular object as to taking Captain G——. The latter was shot, and died almost immediately. Had this happened during the conflict, it might have been correct enough, though rather harsh and unnecessary in an armed police against an individual, for, comparatively, a trifling offence; but as the story is told, it is quite inexcusable, and seems to have been merely an act of spite and vexation, at having suffered themselves to be repulsed by the Captain. It was revenge for having exposed their cowardice.

The fox-hounds were out yesterday, and killed a fox; but had not a very good run. Lord Wellington wore the Salisbury hunt coat, sky-blue and black cape. The Spanish General Frere accompanied him, and as formerly he was a General of cavalry, and the fox soon took to earth, I understand Frere kept up, but all his staff were distanced.

I feel now quite at ease with my animals, as I have collected straw, and hay, and furze enough for about eight days, which is with us looking very forward, as much so as is prudent. My Spanish boy, after being here a day or two, said he would rather set out and try to find his way to Madrid, so I dismissed him, lest he should take a horse or mule to expedite him on his journey, and perhaps a little money, &c., also.

We cannot prevent the Spanish boats from still getting down the Adour to Bayonne, though it is not quite as easy as it was to navigate the river. If all remains quiet, Lord Wellington talks of giving a ball here on the 18th of January, the Queen's birthday, but nothing can be settled long beforehand. The English ladies will be few, and all married ones. We have still only four of the legitimate kind. The mayor of the town says, that a number of the ladies who frequented the balls before we came, and of whom I found a list in my quarter, are still here, and will be forthcoming if called upon.

I find my French " seat of war" a most useful acquisition, as it now contains the whole war, except our own, and that I have in the map of this department, which is on a superior scale.

From four to six our promenade on the wall is

quite gay, for all the great men of business, up to
Lord Wellington himself, generally appear there
at that time, and the Guards also, though the exertion of walking, which we men of business are
used to exercise at a true twopenny postman's long
trot, is too great for them; yet they are formed
about in knots and groups, sitting on the wall, or
gently lounging on it, and though they stop the
way very much, they add to the gaiety of the scene.
We soon perceive when their turn of duty at the
outposts takes them away to the front for a week.

As a proof of the supine inactive state of the
Spanish government, bread and corn are so cheap
and abundant this year in the Castiles, that they
are quite without demand, and it even answers to
bring Spanish bread up here to sell, above fifty, and,
I believe, a hundred miles, and yet the Spanish
nation, relieved from the French army and ours,
cannot supply the few men we have in front with
us, in France, and on the frontier, with money or
anything.   To prevent their plundering, we now
not only have clothed Don Carlos's soldiers, near
Hasparen, but have given them a month's pay,
and ration them with biscuits from England.
With such a nation, and such a population, the
state of the Spanish army, and supplies, which
get, I think, worse instead of better, is most

provokingly disgraceful to their government and
leading men.

I have been much struck with the change in
the appearance of this town, when French head-
quarters and when English. It shows the difference between the two nations. When I was last
there, all was gay and glittering, full of chattering
officers in their best uniforms, with gold lace and
ornaments, and prancing country steeds with hous-
ings and trappings of all kinds. The shops were
crowded with sky-blue and scarlet caps embroidered
with silver and gold, and pantaloons the same, smart
cloaks, trinkets, &c. The road was covered with
long cars, bringing in supplies drawn by mules
gaily ornamented, and with bells, and waggoners
with blue frocks, and long smacking whips, whilst
the quay was nearly deserted, only a few boats to
be seen which had just returned from an unsuccessful attempt to send in shot and shells to St.
Sebastian ; the sailors idle, and scarcely the appearance of a port visible. Bread and vegetables were
abundant ; other eatables, not so.

Now, we have, on the contrary, a different scene ;
not a piece of finery is to be seen, no gay caps, no
pantaloons, no ornaments. The officers all morning in their great coats, Lord Wellington in his
plain blue coat, and round hat, or perhaps in his

sky-blue Salisbury hunting dress. The streets, full of Spanish mules, with supplies, and muleteers, &c., all running against you, and splashing you as you walk; every shop crowded with eatables, wines, sauces, pickles, hams, tongues, butter, and sardines. The quay is now always a busy scene, covered with some rum casks, and flour casks, and suttler stores, the sailors all in our pay, at work constantly and making fortunes, the pilots in full hourly employment, bringing in vessels here or at Sacoa. The latter is full of masts and sails from Passages, Bilboa, Lisbon, or the west of England. The prices are still enormous, and of course the activity is the result. The French peasants are always on the road between this and Bayonne, bringing in poultry, and smuggling out sugar in sacks on their heads.

The Basques must have been a very happy race twenty years since, for though generally a poor country, there is plenty of their food, Indian corn, and excellent meadows by the rivers, which are numerous. Fish is easily procured—the houses are spacious, and comfortable, and the children seem numerous, well-grown, intelligent, and healthy. The men are tall, straight, and active ; the women, stout and useful, and rather good looking. Nor could I see any great deficiency of young men, the proportions seemed much the same as in England, though certainly there are not so many tall idle fellows about as in Ireland. The town, however, had evident marks, I think, of a progress to retrograde and decay.

Later, the 16*th.*—By our last French papers, which we now have to the 8th, and which bring us the good news from Genoa, I find our accounts of Bonaparte setting out to put himself at the head of a hundred and eighty thousand men, near Dijon or Mâcon, is at least premature, as he is still reviewing at Paris. We have stories of disturbances owing to the conscription, but nothing certain seems known about them. The French, a few days since, surprised a few of our forage mules near Lahoupon ; I believe only eight. Lahoupon is a place neither party is fixed in, but both patrole through occasionally.

P.S.—Notwithstanding, Cobbet, as I understand, says, we men from the Peninsula must never think of marrying English women, we may at least be anxious about our friends ; as we are not, I conclude, worn out for friendship, as well as for love, I beg you will tell me all you can, as usual, about every one in your world. Many here are very low after the perusal of that paper, by no means relishing the contents.

CHAPTER XI.

STATE OF FEELING IN FRANCE—ROCKET PRACTICE—THE
PRINCE REGENT'S HOBBY—THE MAYOR'S BALL—THE FLAG-
OF-TRUCE.

Head-Quarters, St. Jean de Luz,
January 15th, 1814.

MY DEAR M——

AFTER two or three days' perpetual rain, we have to-day a clear beautiful day; thermometer in my room at 63°.

In the midst of a terrible storm the day before yesterday arrived a little cockle-shell of a sloop, in our open bay, with the Count de Grammont on board and Colonel Abercrombie, with despatches and a paper of the 10th. This told the leading news. We have thus heard that the Danes are with us; ideas of peace thrown aside, and the Allies across the Rhine. This is popular news here, for almost all are against a peace with Bonaparte, partly from public feelings of such a peace being injurious to England and the world, partly from any peace being not desirable to our military men, especially to those on the staff, whose splendour would be much shorn by it. The civilians and common regimental officers, who are not on the eve of a step, are alone inclined to a peace; to many it will be ruinous.

We again hear of refractory conscripts, and men refusing to march, in the right of the department de Landes and elsewhere, and I believe it in some degree, but this alone will not do without a more general feeling, and even then scarcely, unless a portion of the army takes a part and declares its views against the common enemy Bonaparte, whom all Europe are now hunting like a mad dog.

The Count de Grammont has made a most expeditious trip. He had had communications with the persons on his former property here, and I suppose his visit home was connected with this, to know what line to pursue, &c. The feelings of this part of France seem, as yet, to be still the same; all desire peace, and for that purpose are eager to get rid of Bonaparte, but there is no feeling manifested towards the Bourbons, not as yet, at least; and I really believe the military men, and even many civilians, would rather have Bonaparte if

they could be sure of a peace with him. He has
done much for them, and on a great scale. The
Code Napoleon has been a great work, and from
what I hear is much liked; instead of being governed, in fact, and oppressed by the rich, as they
were before, they are governed by the law, and
that a good law, and as the mayor here and several
others say, well administered, when the state
was not concerned. The only defect seemed to
be that the magistrates having been latterly ill-
paid, there was a temptation to corruption on their
part, and this was a change from anarchy, and
therefore the more felt, as then the strongest (I
mean in means and territory) was everything and
the poor man nothing; in short, the only really
great grievance felt at this distance from the court
of the tyrant seems to have been the horrid conscription and its tremendous increase of late, and
the want of commerce. Nor would the French feel
either of these so much as any other nation in
Europe would do; not the first, on account of the
natural tendency of the inhabitants to a military
life and habits; and not the last, from the great internal resources of France in other respects, making
her feel the loss of commerce much less than almost
any other power which had been accustomed to
enjoy them. I do not mean, therefore, less than

Austria, which has been so generally shut out from commerce to any extent, but as in comparison with England, Holland, Sweden, &c.

Thursday, 20*th.*—Another change again in our weather. Yesterday it was, till one or two o'clock, quite a fine sun-shiny warm day, like our May, and we were all out, seeing some experiments made with the rockets, about two miles off, when a storm gathered, and soon the rain and wind came, and has continued to this time. The night has been tremendous, and one of our Commissariat transports has been on shore in our bay here, stranded, and I fear five or six lives are lost; all hands are now at work moving the stores, corn, and hay.

We had all the military men in the vicinity with Lord Wellington, including General Frere, the Spanish General. The ground-rockets, intended against cavalry, did not seem to answer very well; they certainly made a most tremendous noise, and were formidable spitfires—no cavalry could stand if they came near them, but there seemed the difficulty, none went within half a mile of the intended object, and the direction seemed excessively uncertain. The ground was very bad, and on a flat, or along a road, where they would ricochet or bound along straight they might do very well, but in our case they went bang into the ground, sometimes within two hundred yards, and sometimes one way and sometimes another. Some instead of going fourteen hundred yards, as intended, were off in a hundred, and some pieces of the shell came back even amongst us spectators, one very near Dr. N—— and me, whilst we were standing on one side out of the way as we thought. The fire, however, seemed very strong, as one got into a green hedge, and set it in a blaze directly, the furze and heath were on fire, and only put out by the rain. Those which were let off at an elevation supposed for burning towns, &c., were much better, and some went very near the spot, compared with others; that is, I think they would have hit Bayonne, for instance, somewhere or other, and have set fire to the town I have no doubt; but the part of the town you could not very well choose, as their power seemed very various, and the wind at times carried them three hundred or four hundred yards away from the direction.

Upon the whole I do not think they were much admired, though, in certain cases, they might be useful, especially when the enemy are in a mountainous track, like our Pamplona battle, and near us ; where guns could not well be got up, these rockets could be carried by hand, or on mules, and let off near, would have tremendous effect, even upon infantry when in column. General ——, who is very wise and knowing in the secret views and springs of everything (or at least would be thought so), says, all that fuss of the Crown Prince and Sir C. Stewart, about the effect of the rockets in the North, was to please the Prince Regent in England, the grand patron of the rockets.

The stranded ship was, I hear, driven out of the harbour of Sacoa by the gale. This is quite extraordinary, as the vessels are there quite shut up. The place is, however, too full by far, for no transport likes to move again when once safe there. The packet lost in the harbour of Passages last week shows you the sort of gales and seas we have here.

This morning a French picket of about thirty men were marched off from hence, prisoners; they were surprised by us two nights ago. We got close, and, when challenged, an old Highlander called out " Deserter ;" so the sentinel did not fire, and our fellows got in among them and carried off the picket. I am not very glad of this, for I fear it will lead the French to try and return the compliment, and make the outpost duty much more dangerous and troublesome than it has been. If it only leads to their shooting our next deserter, so much the better. Deserters continue to come in,

and tell strange stories. They say Marshal Soult
has issued orders, that whenever a foreigner is to
be on outpost duty, all his necessaries, knapsack,
&c., are to be taken from him, and he is besides to
be watched and placed with others. They even
say, a German posted as sentry has his shoes taken
away from him. This, barring exaggeration, I
have no doubt is nearly true.

They do say, that last week there were three
hundred young conscripts belonging to one regiment employed to carry bread to the brigade, and
that when near one of the French sentinels, he
challenged them, and as, from not understanding
matters, they made no answer and advanced, he
fired at them, and the whole three hundred threw
down their bread and ran into camp, crying, the
enemy were coming.

But the best story of all, if true, is from the
mayor of Biaretz, who says he understands three
French divisions are under orders to proceed straight
to Lyons, whether to meet Schwartzenburg, or on
account of disturbances, does not seem clear, even
if the story be true.

Friday, January 21st.—In spite of the wet
yesterday, Lord Wellington having heard of the
surprised picket, set off to the front to see about it,
or, as he said last night, to know if it was worth

while to surprise it again, as it has been renewed
by the French ; but he thought not, and was back
here to dinner, and at a ball at the mayoralty in
the evening. This ball was an attempt to see how
far anything of the sort would answer. The
mayor was to manage it, and ask all the ladies ;
and a list of the officers to be asked was given to
him, and tickets sent out, and he was to provide
the best entertainment he could for a dollar a-head
from the gentlemen only, which will be collected
accordingly. It went off, however, but ill, and will
not, I think, be renewed. There were about a
dozen or fifteen elderly women, French, who have
remained here, and who seemed of the better
order, but who came in our country-town fashion,
with the cloak, the woman servant, and the large
lantern, only many of them brought the maid in
with them to sit behind and look on. Then there
were about sixteen or eighteen younger ladies,
French, but who seemed to be nearly all the tradesmen's (quite the shopkeepers') families in the place,
I think none of the better sort, but from behind
the counter in the morning. They were, however,
well dressed, and danced tolerably for French—for
English very finely. About half a dozen old Frenchmen, some respectable ; and about eight young
beaux of the place, who had escaped the conscription,

and who had remained here, made up the French party. There were six English ladies on the whole, but who, excepting one, declined dancing French dances or waltzes, and there was nothing else but one country dance, which went off ill. I have no doubt the French either thought them excessively fine, or that they could not dance. There might be quite as much of the latter as the former. Then to fill up, came about two hundred officers, all in their best, and forming a very smart squeeze. What would your fine ladies in London have not given for such a display of gentlemen. All the field officers of six battalions of the Guards, and about fifty other guards' officers, and all the head-quarters' staff, generals, aides-de-camp, &c., were there.

I think Cobbet would have admitted that, with so many fine young men there, the whole Peninsula squad could not be quite so despicable in the eyes of the English fair. Three sets of cotillions were formed, and some waltzes, but the whole went off but indifferently. A Frenchman of about forty or fifty, one of the police of the town, volunteered a hornpipe, which was tolerably good. About 12 or 1 o'clock, there was a long table opened for the ladies, covered with pastry of different shapes, no meat—the wine, claret. At half-past

one I came away, leaving the dancers rather beginning to romp. I think it will not do, because
the belles are not good enough to please in a sober
way, and if liberties are taken they would be
offended, or at least their male relations would be
for them. Lord Wellington was soon off, and
whilst there seemed to be principally occupied with
little military arrangements. He, however, seemed
pleased with the thing, and asked me as I passed,
if I thought Gazan ever had a better ball? I only
said, "I am sure there never were so many gentlemen in the mayor's house before." Better dancing,
however, there may have been.

Still rain, without ceasing. I have been skip-
ping with one of my mule ropes, instead of my
walk to-day with my umbrella. I got to the wrecked
ship yesterday. The best account seems to be,
that she pulled up the post to which she was
fastened in Sacoa harbour, and drifted out; the
Captain was on shore, the missing are three men
and a woman, and they are supposed lost, and it is
believed the men were in the rigging trying to
make things right, when the mast broke. The
Guards were set to work as fatigue parties at low
water, and the cargo removed on shore, consisting
of hay and biscuit, and not much damaged by the
wreck. The hay, however, of which one truss fell

to my share, was previously almost mouldy with wet, perhaps a little taste of salt may give it a relish, and anyhow it is as good as coarse straw and furze, and better than nothing, which is my mules' long forage at present. The muleteer is so popular, the Portuguese give him so much drink to make him dance and amuse them, that he is very ill with it, and lying below with a blister and emetic; and the mules therefore get no grass, as I cannot turn them out; and straw I cannot afford them.

I have just heard another curious trick of the French here. They advanced towards Murillo's Spaniards,—the latter fired at them; they sent in to say they were very much surprised, for they understood they were at peace with the Spaniards now, as a treaty was signed. Murillo sent back for answer, that he knew of no peace, and if the Cortes or Regency had signed such a peace, still he should continue to do as the English did, and fire at the French until orders came to him to the contrary, and that regularly through the Duke of Ciudad Rodrigo. This is all as it should be, but the trick is a curious one.

Saturday, *22nd*.—Our weather is now more like winter than it has yet been; at St. Jean de Luz we have a raw, cold air, no sun, a damp fog. La Rune and all the hills round are covered with snow; nothing but a little sleet has fallen here.

Sunday, Post-day.—A fine day, but really like winter, the coldest we have had, and a north-east wind, which will, I think, before it arrived here, have frozen you all up stiff in England and in Holland. We were all yesterday surprised by the news that the French pickets were all withdrawn near Bayonne on our front on this side, and that we might proceed close in to the works round Bayonne. What this means exactly we none of us know; Lord Wellington, however, was over immediately, to have a peep into the town on that side. Careless about himself, he got so close, that I understand there were some French in a house within about forty yards of him, and he did not move until he thought a French frigate, lying in the harbour, seemed to be making some preparations, as if going to fire at the party. As I mentioned to you, it was on the 10th of December, in front here, he got quite in the midst of the broken Portuguese, where there were cross fires on all sides, and was fearful on moving off quickly back, even though he wanted to go and order up fresh troops, lest the bad example might increase the disorder, and make the men in greater confusion; so he went leisurely back, until out of sight, and then cantered off to the unbroken part of the column.

We have more reports of insurrections in France, and the French have been circulating the story, that the preliminaries of peace (a general peace) are already signed, and have sent the report in here. I suspect it is all a trick, as all shifts and schemes are now resorted to ; amongst others, Bonaparte has sent back Palafox to Spain—it is concluded, to intrigue, as he is well known now, and the Cortes have, I am told, refused to receive him or take any notice of him. The promotion of O'Donaghue as Lieutenant-general, and his quitting the situation of War Minister in consequence, is considered as a sort of triumph on our part, as he was suspected of being inimicable to Lord Wellington and the British interests. His successor, Moreno, I know nothing of, except that he has generally been of the War Council, and in civil-military employments, and has not seen much service.

Head-Quarters, St. Jean de Luz, January 26, 1814.—I have now another letter to thank you for, of the date of the 11th instant, and papers to the same period, for which my best thanks are due. These arrived by the sloop of war, with Colonel

Bunbury, and are particularly acceptable, for (excepting Lord Wellington) no one has letters by the packet or papers later than the 5th. Colonel Bunbury brought one of the 13th for Lord Wellington. In some degree, however, all your papers now lose their interest, as we have a sort of information through Paris, very much quicker, and though not very much to be depended upon, and not very full or accurate, yet it gives us, making all due allowances, a tolerable insight into what is passing. We have thus now papers of the 17th from Paris, from which it appears the Allies have been at Besançon, Dijon, and even Langres, whilst your accounts only carry them to the frontiers of Switzerland.

The deficiency of my Spanish maps does not signify, for I merely sent them home as a sort of memorial of Vittoria. All I had were only about the tenth part of Lopez, and nearly one-half of what I had are gone to the bottom in the little *Catherine,* in which I sent two parcels.

General G—— was always here famous for hospitality and very large parties. The only objection was the too great crowd at dinner. From what I saw, however, I liked him extremely. There was a wide distance between him and Lord Wellington in material points for a Commander-in-Chief, though I believe he was more popular with those under him, and particularly with his staff.

You need never apologize for forwarding a letter by any officer sent out express in a ship of war, and direct to head-quarters, as that is the best of all conveyances when available, as they are sure to use the greatest expedition, and to have the best sailing-vessel. An officer coming out with convoy in a transport to join his regiment is quite *une autre chose*, and to be as much avoided.

We have, for the last three days, had a touch of your late weather, and have had snow on the ground over to the sea's edge every night fresh, and remaining all day on the ground. It is still not very cold in reality, and indeed less so than I could wish it, as I think if colder, we should feel it less. This seems paradoxical, but the truth is, the ground here is not hard, and the snow when trodden upon in the streets, melts, and forms a most chilling mud, and there is a cold evaporation going on worse than a hard frost. It is here every day like our first beginning of a cold thaw. I have, unluckily, one Portuguese in the hospital with typhus, and one in bed, that is confined to the fern in the stable, with a bowel complaint, but I rub on somehow.

Yesterday I had one of my deputies, passing through here, to dinner. He is a very gentleman-like, quiet, and most diligent character, and I only hope my mention of him, in particular to General Pakenham, the Adjutant-general, coupled with that of Colonel Royals, whose Adjutant he has been, may do him some service. He has been down at Coimbra, and elsewhere. His name is Arden, a Lieutenant of the 61st. He was last from St. Andar, and told me a curious story about a late flag-of-truce there.

Much of our clothing was, you may have heard, carried to Santona, near there, as a prize. Many of our men were, consequently, in absolute tatters. Lord Wellington proposed to Soult to buy it at a valuation, and let the Governor of Santona have the money to pay his garrison. Soult agreed, and gave an order, with a pass. Mr. Drake, the Commissary, was ordered to go into Santona, in consequence, with a flag to treat. Instead of one trumpeter—five persons improperly went with him. The officer on the post (a French one), came out, told him he did not understand a flag-of-truce with five persons, and the Spaniards drawn up so near, that he might uspect treachery, and must do his duty, though Soult's orders and pass might be all reguiar. In short he said, " I return in, and in one minute, I fire a gun at you ; so make the best of your way off. Though the party offered to be

taken in as prisoners, the Frenchman went in—so
off they ran ; and just as they turned the corner
of a house, a twenty-four pounder was after them.
The Governor was angry with the officer. A new
flag with one person advanced : Drake was admitted, but was blinded for nearly a league ; and
yet the person with him, and another, let in afterwards, were permitted to see all. When the mission
was understood, and the parties discovered to be
civilians, the Governor was very polite. He gave
them good wine, &c., but bad bread and meat, which,
I think, the power of fancy made Drake think was
horse-flesh. He then said that the shoes, gaiters,
pantaloons, and some of the caps, his men then had
in use, so that, as to those, the mission was too late ;
but the jackets they were welcome to purchase,
with some other things, and a bargain was soon
made. The Governor then said, " I know your
road home is infamous to St. Andar—you shall return in our privateer row-barge." This they did
in a very short time, and the finale was a formal
complaint from the Spanish authorities at St. Andar,
against Drake, for having dared to let a French
row-boat enter St. Andar without their leave and
their pass. When in the town, all the children,
&c., crowded round Drake and his party to see an
Englishman. This made the Governor very angry

and he had them dispersed, asking them, "what there was to look at in an Englishman?" at which they shouted under his nose—" *Viva los Ingleses !* *Viva, Viva !*" I wish the higher class of Spaniards were as staunch as the peasantry and rabble.

Saturday.—Our regular mail has not yet arrived ; so your papers up to the 11th have been in most constant request, for, though there was one here up to the 13th, there was no regular set to the 11th. Our snow has ended in torrents of cold rain again ; the roads, almost more impassable, if that be possible, than they were before, of course impede all movement, even if intended. Nothing but a rising, commotions, &c., would tempt us out, and that must be without cannon in a great measure, and dependant for provisions principally on the country, as our transport diminishes daily in the army, from the death of mules, or desertion of muleteers.

The life just now of the subaltern officers is a very arduous and unpleasant one ; winter-quarters they certainly have, but that is all ; four or five in a room, comforts very few, a great deal of duty with forage parties, and going to Passages for corn, bread, &c., and always in the wet, and up to the knees in mud. The business, however, must I think end soon.

We have French papers to the 20th, and thus find the Allies at Langres, Dijon, and Lyons; we are told they are well received. Upon this it must very much turn at last. The news from the French camp and from Bayonne is of peace. Our mayor has had a letter from his confidential friend at Bayonne. The basis was at last agreed upon on both sides, and a congress to take place at Basle. This may be fabricated, for the purpose of keeping the country and army here quiet until the event be really so. The French must now or never get rid of Bonaparte, if they wish it. It is not very flattering to the Bourbons, that even the repeated sufferings and disasters the nation has endured from Bonaparte scarcely seem to be able to rouse up the least attachment to them; and that even the last necessity seems hardly to make the people willing to run any risks for their old family; and yet I am almost sure the feeling would rapidly spread from the sort of despair now prevailing as to *la pauvre France*, if a good beginning could but once be made.

You must remember the article of capitulation as to the *Commissaire de Guerre* and his family, the brother's wife, and two daughters, &c., at St. Sebastian. They have never yet returned to

France, and are now here. The exchange of the *Commissaire* could never be arranged; and the ladies, though offered to return without him, would not do so, expecting that he would every day be able to accompany them. Lord Wellington let them remain at Passages, until the matter was finally settled; and there they have been all the time in the same house with one of our Commissaries, Mr. M——. And now when they were all to go back, the latter has declared himself the admirer professed of the youngest girl, and they are after all halted here at St. Jean de Luz until he can marry her, and then the rest of the party pass into the French lines. I met them at dinner yesterday; they are a pleasant family. The girl pleasing, and rather pretty, and in the English style; the mother a clever woman; the other girl not pretty, but odd, and, I think, clever.

Our new Admiral is arrived, having left England on the 21st. All our mails are thus forestalled, as we have still only mail papers and letters to the 5th. We are told there is no news in particular, but that all is warlike. Our story here is, however, of a still later date, and may possibly still be true. The only other news we have is from Catalonia; and that, I fear, is bad. You will, however, get it before you have this, I conclude, from the *Gazette*. General Donkin told me his letters said we had made an attack on Moulins del Rey on the Lobregat, near Barcelona; that the Spaniards were to cross the river and turn the French; that they were too slow and too late, and so the whole plan failed; but that we suffered but little, and that the loss was nearly all Spanish, who lost two colonels—killed. I do not believe all Spain would drive Suchet or his army out, except by time, and wear and tear—never by force. The government, however, have behaved well, I believe, as to the late French attempts, through Ferdinand and through our English hero, Palafox.

I am sorry not to be able still to admire the latter. It is mortifying to strike out the name of one of the few Spanish heroes this five years' war has produced. I am now, however, satisfied that we owe the Spanish insurrection, and all its good consequences, to the thorough ignorance and want of calculation, and of information, and of judgment of the Spaniards. If they had more common sense, and knowledge of the true state of things, even their zeal and patriotism (which I admit were considerable) would never have induced them to adopt a course so devoid of all prospect of a

N 3

favourable result, and which every thinking, impartial, able man must have pronounced a desperate mad scheme. We owe it principally, I am sure, to their excessive pride and ignorance, their good opinion, yet want of knowledge of themselves. And this accounts for the most able men at first all going the wrong way.

Sunday, 30th, post-day.—Nothing but wind and rain, wind and rain for ever, and no more news! Some of the deserters say the French head-quarters are removed to my old place, Mont de Marsan ; but I should think scarcely, as yet. The new admiral dined at head-quarters yesterday, but, I understand, has brought little news. I fear he has lost one ship under his orders already, as we have a report of a sloop-of-war, *The Holly*, lost at Passages, and several of the crew with it. This is certainly a terrible coast. There is now a vessel riding in our bay, very uneasy, and cannot enter ; and one was as nearly as possible lost yesterday morning close to Sacoa : the surf broke over her. The exertions of the French pilots were astonishing.

Sunday, later, 5 o'clock, 30th.—Business prevents my adding more, and indeed I have nothing to add. We have two French officers come out here from England to see after a better fate by a little *intrigo*, I suppose. One is a Basque of this country, on half-pay from our service, and the other, a Monsieur La Fitte, I believe a clever man, and a La Vendee hero.

CHAPTER XII.

ARMY SUPPLIES—OFFENDING VILLAGES—SYMPTOMS OF WORK
—ARRIVAL OF THE DUKE D'ANGOULEME—THE BRIDGE
ACROSS THE ADOUR—WELLINGTON AND HIS CHIEF ENGI-
NEER—HIS ACTIVITY.

Head-Quarters, St. Jean de Luz,
February 2nd, 1814.

MY DEAR M——

HERE we remain absolutely tied by the leg
by the horrible state of the roads, and weather,
and without any regular news from England,
Nothing but reports on the side of France which
would encourage us to proceed ; and, on the sea-
side, of heavy gales, and lost vessels. I am just
now driven in by a furious hailstorm, and yet the
weather is mild, and, till this moment, pleasant
enough. We have two ships in our little bay, one
full of hay, which has been four days nearly within
three hundred yards of the shore, and in hourly
danger of drifting on the beach ; and yet we have
not been able, in spite of our distress, to get out a

truss ; and the other a brig transport, empty, and driven in here against her will by stress of weather. A frigate was also off here all yesterday, apparently labouring much, and fearful of the coast. We certainly have undertaken a bold thing in winter- ing in such a place, but it was a choice of diffi- culties.

If we had money we should do well, but that is as scarce as anything else. Plenty of supplies would come in from the right from the French had we cash to give in return. As it is, in consequence of the little ready money we gave at first, a great quantity of cattle, food, &c., has been obtained, but now we are reduced to Treasury bills, and that cannot last, and the loss is very great. Even the muleteers get a past payment now in those bills, and the consequence is that a person may buy them with dollars at the rate of 7s. 4d., and, I believe, 7s. 6d. a dollar. The army is also six months, and the staff seven months in arrear of their pay.

We have, however, I believe, plenty of bread and biscuit, and meal for a month with the army, and corn at Passages in abundance. The short transport from thence is almost too much for us, and the supply is by no means general to the animals, whilst long forage is quite a rarity. The destruc-

tion of the oxen is frightful in the rear. Our great
depôt is as far back as Palencia, and even there,
in store, the cattle die very fast, and the moment
they march they fall away to nothing, and die by
fifties. Our Commissary-general almost despairs
of getting more up, although he has made depôts
of bran and straw, &c., on the road, to try and
obviate the total want of food. It is now in con-
templation to ship cattle from St. Andar, where
there is a store ; but then we have rather a scarcity
of naval transports also. Cattle would come in as
fast as we wished from twenty leagues to our
right, could we but pay for it. As it is, I am
almost inclined to think we shall, as a choice of
evils, be obliged in spite of the roads, &c., to move
towards our right in quest of food.

Two of the villages in that direction have justly
incurred Lord Wellington's displeasure by plundering and seizing our forage parties, of which we
have lately lost several. One or two were taken
by the peasants of those two villages, and Lord
Wellington has issued a proclamation addressed
to them and that country, saying, he told them
before to remain at home, and be quiet, and to
take no part, and he would protect them, but that
he would not have this treachery in return. If
they did not like this proposal, well and good,

then let them quit their *foyers* and leave their villages, and take the consequence, and he should be prepared to meet them as enemies ; but they must make this election. The curé of one of these villages was carried off as a hostage for their good behaviour in future. We have strong reports of commotions and internal dissatisfactions in France, and that Bonaparte is reduced to concentrate his army round Paris. If this be true, Lord Wellington must be half mad about the roads. I find he is gone out to day to look about him. Two ninepounders have just drawn up opposite my windows with eight horses each, and the men have left their guns under the charge of the Provost guard. I suppose they are on the march. I must inquire what this means.

February 3rd.—The artillery is said to mean nothing ; but still I think if we get fine weather for a week we shall have a start. In confirmation of what I have written above, as to the loss of cattle, I will give you two instances: three hundred and sixty head of convalescent bullocks, which had been left at Vittoria to get into order, were marched for the army ; sixty only have arrived thus far, all the rest have been left at stations between, or been given to the different alcaldes, and receipts taken for them—a new mode lately adopted. Five hundred of another lot of fresh ones, collected at Palencia, were marched all this way, three hundred only have reached Vittoria, and all the bad road and scarcity of food is yet to come. This is really quite alarming.

February 3rd, later.—I find my guns mean nothing ; they are only going on to the front to replace two now there, which are to come back to refit. Still, however, if we could but get fine weather, I think we should make a stir. Bets were going on as to a peace, or our being at Bayonne and across the Adour in six weeks ; and I think I see symptoms of a move soon. The rain, however, continues. Colonel Bunbury made one attempt to go to the right of our army the day before yesterday, but only got half-way, and is unwell in consequence. He is to leave this either in Lord Wellington's carriage or to go round by water to Passages. The sea is, however, quiet, and now only torments our anxious curiosity by throwing up parts of wrecks and bodies. A ship-cable, with the G.R., was found at Bidart, and three men and a woman. Some say the latter had silk stockings on. One body cast up here was half eaten, and I saw a back-bone only yesterday. The bodies of the mules float in and out every tide.

As a proof of the state of forage here, and of

the manner in which we are imposed upon, five shillings were yesterday demanded for a sack of chopped furze from the surrounding hills, and thus sold in the market. Straw fetches two shillings for a small handful, which a horse would eat two or three of in a day.

I have just seen a Spanish Captain who was taken prisoner a little more than three months since. He has been to Mâcon since, on the Saone, where the Allies now are, about six hundred miles from this, having been first plundered of his great coat and pantaloons. He was about thirty-five days getting there on foot all the way, staid there forty days, and then was about thirty-six days more returning here, also on foot, having been exchanged. He says the notion is, we have the Duke d'Angoulême here, and that very many wish it to be so. This is like my finding many persuaded we had the Duke de Berri with our army when I was a prisoner. I suspect, however, we shall in part verify this notion now, as I just hear one of the best quarters in the town is to be cleared immediately for an unknown great man, now at Passages, and just arrived from England. At first they even talked of moving the Adjutant-general, Pakenham, to make room for him. This mystery will, however, soon be cleared up. Rain,

which is never pleasant, was never so disagreeable
as now.   The fate of France may depend upon it.
I am vexed all the while I hear its patter about
me.

The owner of my house is a well-bred woman,
who lives in a great house opposite. She lives in
one corner of it, whilst General Wimpfen and his
staff, and Colonel M——, his wife, and three
children, occupy all the best part. She has, she
told me, thirteen houses round here, five are burnt,
and two coming down, and yet she seems resigned
and satisfied that we have really behaved very
well, that it is the fate of war, and owing to the ill
fortune of having property in a frontier country
near armies, and is quite inevitable. She only
exclaims, *"Oh la pauvre France!"* This is a
novel language to the French of late.

4th, Friday. Still rain, rain, rain, all night.
All yesterday, all the night before, and still continuing. Oh ! that we had your frost instead ; all
things would have been very different.

The great man just arrived, and now here, turns
out to be the Duke d'Angoulême, and Count
Damas is come out with him ; but till the plot
thickens, the Duke is *incog.*

Our pontoons from the Bidassoa, are now passing
over the St. Jean de Luz bridge.   This looks like

something, and we have to-day at last, a dry day, or at least a half day, as I must not be too sure yet. The wind is getting round to the north a little, or north-east, and if that remains it will do, especially as it is full moon; though I must say I have not much more faith in the moon, in respect of weather, than Lord Wellington has, who says it is nonsense. In addition to all your news, we have French news of a battle at St. Dizier, near Chalons, and that the Allies have been beaten. I fear it is not all to go as smooth as hitherto, unless a rising takes place.

All odd strangers who come to head-quarters here have been long called tigers. Of course we now have " The Royal Tiger." This is a head-quarters joke for you. We have had for some time here a Madame de ——, the wife of the Commandant of ——, come to make arrangements before-hand, and here she certainly has been making many little arrangements not much to the advantage of her husband, and not quite consistent with conjugal fidelity. When the Commandant arrived yesterday, at last, she immediately began to blame him for his unnecessary delay, &c., and insinuated that another lady was the cause. This is very hard upon a poor old man, but I suppose the lady thought it right to take the initiative.

The publication of the Leipsig letters, which George mentions, of Murray's, will be very curious, but I think it is not right to let these be published. Similar letters were taken in Spain more than once, and police reports. The old letters which were too late (those I mean from you) were from the Secretary of State's office, not from the Judge-Advocate's office. I suspect they were mislaid at the former.

Sunday, post-day.—Bright sun, and a smiling sky, with a smooth bay covered with ships, quite a Vernet, and I am just returned from the church service on the beach, in a square of about two thousand five hundred guards, and all the staff here present. As I returned, I picked up your letter of the 26th, and papers at the post-office. I do not recollect anything particular to answer, and have just got some business come in, as desertion has commenced again now we are quiet and idle. A corporal and twelve men all went off together a few nights since, all foreigners, and I believe French. Our people at home are very careless in selecting soldiers to enlist into our corps from the prisons. What can be better for a Frenchman in a prison-ship than to receive 4*l.*, new clothes, arms, &c., and then to be sent into his own country, and put in a situation to join his comrades,

with only the difficulty of watching a good occasion
to join them. In yesterday's return, however, nine
men have deserted, mostly English. Your English
news is all good, as far as it goes, and if this weather
will but hold a little, I think you will hear of more
glory and more broken heads here. In addition
to the pontoons which have passed up, scaling
ladders have gone through here. If we could but
cross the mouth of the Adour below Bayonne, and
get at the citadel at once by scaling and storm,
there would be something like a blow, and the
town would be at our mercy immediately.

We have some gentlemen here, but very few,
who begin to find the work too warm for them.
I have been saved two cases of this sort, very
awkward ones, by resignations, and have been
consulted on two others by General Cole, very
suspicious ones, but not as clear as the other two
who are let off thus, to save the reputation of the
regiments. An officer should think a little before
he engages in service, such as we have had here
the last few years.

More business, so I must put an end to this
quickly. I have not seen the Royal Tiger, but
dine at head-quarters to-day, and hope to do so.
The French ladies are staunch Bonapartists. They
say we shall have another Quiberon business, and

that the Allies are coming into France the same old road as twenty years since, and will return by it. Remember me to all friends.

I have been so pressed to change my old mare, which was in high condition, that, to oblige Major D——, of the Guards, I have done so, and taken Mother Goose (a pet name of General Hulse's formerly) in exchange, and fifteen guineas to boot. Mother Goose is a very good mare, but never would stand fire. She is not as large or showy as my old lady, but I like her much. She was valued at eighty-five guineas, and has always sold for that. I put mine at a hundred guineas. I gave more— four hundred dollars ; as dollars cannot be had under 7s., and the exchange is still higher on the muleteer Treasury bills. These, however, I should not think it right to deal in.

Head-Quarters, St. Jean de Luz, Thursday, February 10th, 1814.— I have arrived thus far in the week, without commencing my usual Journal to you, having had a return of business, and also several gentlemen to swear, and certificates and affidavits to make out, to enable friends to take out administration in England to deceased officers' estates. We have also again had two fine days, and I have been able to get a ride or two in consequence. On Sunday, at head-quarters, I met

the Royal Tiger at dinner—the Duke d'Angoulême—and Monsieur Damas.

Before dinner I got into conversation with the
Duke, without knowing who he was, as they were
both dressed alike in a fancy uniform, very like our
navy Captain's undress, a plain blue coat, with two
gold epaulettes. He seemed much pleased with
his prospects, and very sanguine as to the result.
The day was fine ; he was sure the weather would
last a month. I said the natives told me we should
have rain, and no settled weather until March was
half over. He was sure I had been misinformed.
The fact was, however, that it rained half that very
night, and the whole of the next day. Every day
he expected to proceed into France, and saw all
difficulties vanish. " *Les pauvres conscripts de
Bayonne fondaient comme la neige ; ils etoient
presque tous à l'hôpital,*" and so on.

That we shall make a dash soon, unless peace
prevents it, I fully believe from all I see and hear;
and an embargo which has been laid on all small
vessels in our river confirms this. We have also
to-day an order for twelve days' hay at Passages,
for which we are to send to the ships ourselves, as
Government have just now sent us out a good lot
of English hay, and if we march it must be all left
behind, for we have no means of carrying it with

us. At least the animals will thus all start with a
belly full, which is something, and to many a
novelty.

I do not think much of the little Duke; his
figure and manners are by no means imposing, and
I think his talents are not very great. He seems
affable and good-tempered; and though not seem-
ingly a being to make a kingdom for himself, he
may do very well to govern one when well established. Lord Wellington was in his manner droll
towards them. As they went out, we drew up on
each side, and Lord Wellington put them first;
they bowed and scraped right and left so oddly,
and so actively, that he followed with a face much
nearer a grin than a smile.

They were at church on Sunday, but I cannot
learn with any effect; as yet we cannot judge, for
this small corner dare not speak out their minds if
in his favour. We hear of a strong disposition at
Bordeaux and in Brittany. I have as yet seen
only apathy and indifference; but I still expect a
burst if the war last.

I must now to Lord Wellington about a poor
old Doctor, who has been charged with having a
soldier servant. I expect a jobation for what I
shall state in his favour, as this is a very heinous
offence in the eyes of Lord Wellington.

Same day, later.—Lord Wellington, as I supposed, insisted on the Doctor's being tried, but was
good-humoured, though just going out with the
hounds, when, in general, he does not like inter-
ruption. This particular Doctor had a right to a
servant of his own regiment; but he had one of
another. I suggested that he had never joined his
own regiment since he was appointed, and could
not, therefore, have one of that corps. " Then he
should have gone without," was the answer; and
as for the doctor's good character, that went for
nothing. Lord Wellington never attends to individual hardships, but to the general good; and as
many abuses go on at depôts in the rear, every
time he catches at an instance he is inexorable in
trying to punish, and especially when he finds it
out himself, as he did this, in another trial of the
same poor Doctor, by some of the evidence. The
Doctor, foolish man, desired it might be put on the
minutes that he would ask such a witness no question, as he had been his servant at the time, and
was so still.

I have just heard an anecdote which shows
strongly the Spanish character, and also why Lord
Wellington likes Colonel Dickson as his chief
artillery officer. On the 9th of November last the
order was given for the troops to march to the

attack at four the next morning. This was when we were at Vera. Every one had known for weeks this was to take place the moment it was possible, and that the fall of Pamplona and better weather were the only reasons of the army being in such a position as we then were, perched up on the sides of all the mountains so late in the year, with the prospect of snow daily. At nine that night General Frere, the Spanish General, who is considered as one of their best, sent word that the Spanish army under his command was without any ammunition, and could not get any up in time. At ten o'clock Dickson was sent for, just as he was going to bed; instead of saying nothing could be done, or making any difficulties, he proposed giving the Spaniards immediately the reserve ammunition of the nearest English division, and said he would send out orders instantly, and undertake to get the English reserve replaced in time, and this was done.

Poor E—— got a very loud discourse all the way home from church last Sunday. The oxen of the pontoon train were all dying, and in cross roads were useless, as they could not move singly, except with difficulty, much less draw a pontoon of two tons weight. It had been reported in consequence that three troops of artillery must be dis-

mounted, to draw the pontoon. Lord Wellington
was vexed excessively. " Where are the pontoon
horses ?" " None were ever sent out from England; never had anything but oxen, and five
hundred have died since we left Frenada." This
answer still did not satisfy him. He must, notwithstanding, have known it from the returns
which he sees, but still he seemed, though he
could not tell why, to think poor E—— blameable.
The latter said he had no orders to send to England for horses, and no one seemed to think they
would be necessary, and he had never had them.

Friday 11*th.*—I went last night to our third
ball, in hopes of seeing the Duke d'Angoulême
there, and to observe how he was received. He
did not attend. All our other great men were
there—Lord Wellington and all the French, as yet
very few in numbers. The owner of General
Cole's quarters near Ustaritz, I believe named
Larrique, was there. He had come over to pay his
respects to the Bourbons. He was always royally
disposed, and had been once imprisoned for this
inclination. I am told several others have been to
the Duke to pay their respects merely, but this
is all they dared do as yet. They assure him the
landholders and peasantry further on only wait our
advance, and the absence of the French army, to

rise and declare for the Bourbous. If they do not take this line soon, and that decidedly, peace may make it too late, and frustrate all these petty plans of counter-revolution in the bud. The Duke seems quite ignorant of the people here, and of the country, and those Basques I have talked to do not seem to know much more of him. The few squires left may, however, give the tone to the rest.

I hear we have quite ruined Bayonne market by our higher prices, &c., and things are not only dear there, but not to be had, as no one will there give the price we do for luxuries, as poultry, vegetables, &c., certainly are ; and therefore they are brought here.

Saturday 12*th.*—Our news now is, that Soult and about three thousand infantry, and one thousand eight hundred cavalry, are gone off to the rear, and it seems to be believed ; for it has come through so many channels to us. Another report is, that seven of the thirty tyrants (senators) have gone over to the Allies, to pay their respects to the Bourbons ; this is not in such credit as the other story. In short, we have what the military men call " shaves" (I suppose barbers' stories) every day and every hour. The best fact I can tell you is, that we have had three days fine weather now together, and this last is absolutely warm, I only fear too warm to last; thermometer in my room, window open, and no fire, 58° in the sun. I rode a league out and back yesterday almost without a splash. The mule roads across the country, though improved, are, however, still very bad; three more such days will, nevertheless, do wonders, and about that time I hope we shall be ready.

All the carpenters, &c., are ordered from the Guards to the front. The Rocket Brigade also went up last night, and ships are ordered round from Passages. Dr. Macgregor, who was there yesterday, tells me he thinks it will be three days before they will have procured ropes, &c., and all they require with them. This smiling sun makes every one cheerful, though it prognosticates many broken heads.

The only thing I think the Guards look blue about, is the prospect of an aquatic expedition. Our sick, though nothing compared to last year, have increased this last month, and to show you how much depends on seasoning them, there are two regiments, the 84th, and, I think, 62nd, who came out two months since, and have had no work scarcely, but arrived after all the bad quarters in the mountains, and have not marched forty miles, and been generally housed, and yet are absolutely unfit for the field. One has four hundred and more sick out of six hundred. They are obliged, in consequence. to be sent in a body, as regiments, to Verra, one of the hospital stations. They are, I believe, two battalions, and mostly young lads or elderly men, neither of which class of soldiers can stand this work at all. Some of our old regiments have scarcely a man in the hospital, except the wounded, and it is astonishing how well some of the Portuguese regiments stand it, who are more exposed than our men. The last month's rest, and the new clothes, which most regiments have now received, will revive the army amazingly; some who are still without their clothes are, to be sure, absolutely in rags, or like the king of the beggars.

Head-Quarters, St. Jean de Luz, Sunday the 13*th, post-day,* 5 *o'clock.*—I have been bothered writing from eight this morning until this time, and have only time to seal up, so adieu. Our "shave" of to-day is a Congress. Yesterday the Allies were at Paris, &c. I am sorry to say the sea has risen, and the wind changed, and the weather threatens again. All are hard at work, however, at the bridges, &c. It will be a ticklish thing to cross at the mouth of the Adour.

Head-Quarters, St. Jean de Luz, February 15*th,* 1814.—The plot now thickens a little. Lord Wellington was off at three in the morning yester-

day for Hasparran, for two or three days, to super-
intend a movement which is to take place : first,
on our right, to drive the French divisions of
General Foy and Harispe across the Gave d'Oleron,
and prevent their molesting our right flank, whilst
the passage of the Adour is attempted on the left.
The accounts this morning are, that the troops
assembled for this purpose yesterday, but that no
affair has as yet taken place. General Pakenham
was yesterday at Passages to see to the shipping, &c.,
there, and clear out the hospital ; and to-day he is
gone over to the right, to report to Lord Wellington
and to assist there. All is in motion : two bridges
are preparing, one, as I supposed, below Bayonne,
and another above ; the former will be accompanied
by an aquatic expedition.

With regard to this grand bridge, a most provoking occurrence has taken place.—About twenty-
four vessels were all embargoed in the St. Jean de
Luz river, to form this bridge, and to assist in the
conveyance of troops, &c. Old Ocean, however,
did not approve, and as he is not under Lord Wellington's orders, and seems like the Spaniards to like
to thwart Lord Wellington a little, he (Old Ocean)
threw up the day before yesterday such a mound of
shingle at the mouth of the river, that he has most
effectually embargoed the whole shipping, and made

a dry bank, a hundred feet wide quite firm across the entrance, which all yesterday was used as a road backwards and forwards from Sibour to this place. From the present state of the tides there was no prospect of an opening in the natural way for a week and more, until the springs; so to-day a fatigue party of the Guards are at work digging and shovelling.

In my early walk this morning I found them at it, with a young engineer officer, doing it, as I thought, very ill. I could not help meddling; however, I had no weight, until an old Frenchman came, sent by the mayor, to whom I advised their applying, and then, as the young engineer did not understand French, I acted as interpreter, found the old man's plan and mine agreed, and I carried my point. It is hoped we shall be able to dig a way through by this evening, and to-morrow to let the shipping out. It has never happened before since we have been here, though very often the river is nearly dry.

We have one brig of war arrived, and the *Gleaner* ketch, and Lieutenant Douglas is on shore here superintending the fastening together of a quantity of masts, &c., to form a boom, I believe, across the Adour, I suppose to prevent anything floating down from destroying the bridge. I heard yesterday what one can scarcely believe, that the naval officer asked leave to survey the mouth of the Adour, but that Lord Wellington told him to go to the engineers, and they would give him plans and soundings, &c. ; that he went to E——— accordingly, and found he had none at all ; and Toffini's coast stops short at Passages !

It is surely very odd, now that we have been in front of Bayonne for three months, that no plans should have been sent out, without being asked for from England. I since have heard from E——— that he did write, and has nothing in consequence but a little printed plan of Bayonne, and no soundings, &c. I trust still that Lord Wellington will poke out his way across. Our outposts' reports to-day are : Cossacks close to Paris, and Fontainebleau pillaged by them. I am sorry for that, as that palace escaped the Revolution almost entirely. The truth of the whole story may well be questioned.

February 16*th.*—No news from the right ; no one returned yet ; the reports are, that the French do not stand, but retire before us. In the meantime, things are going on well here. The weather is fine again, the sea quiet, the river has quite cleared his course, and to-day the navigation is open. The fort at the mouth of the Adour sent a few shots against the *Lyra* brig when cruising yesterday to inspect, but no harm done. Every one is busy.

Poor —— does not seem to draw well with Lord Wellington. The latter received him so queerly at the last interview that —— says he shall do all he can to execute what he is ordered, and be quiet. Lord Wellington never consulted him, and has never even told him exactly where the grand bridge which he is preparing is to be, and the consequence is, the width of the river has not been precisely ascertained at the place intended, where the engineers have instruments which would do it in a minute, if they were ordered. Without orders they cannot, as it would require a guard of three hundred or four hundred men to go near enough, and that can only be with orders. But then, were I ——, I should ask for the guard and do it, propose it first, or try and get it quietly from the Adjutant-general without troubling Lord Wellington, and let him find the thing done. —— seems to be too much of the English official school, has too much regard to forms and regular orders. All this *entre nous*. Elphinstone of the Engineers tells me he wrote for a plan of Bayonne four months since, and has only received a very miserable one, almost of no use.

The grand bridge is to be formed of the largest vessels now in the harbour,—about fifty of them. Pontoons would never do. They are to be about 25 feet or 27 feet apart, and cable bridges between to communicate with planks, each vessel carrying its own materials to plank, &c. This is a grand plan, but rather an arduous one. I hope it may answer, as it will be an event in military matters, crossing a great river at the mouth below the fortified town, and that in the hands of the enemy on both sides of the river.

February, 17th, Thursday.—Still fine weather, and no one returned, and no news from Lord Wellington. I had a report here through the emigrés and *son Altesse Royale*, as he is now called, that the Allies are within a league of Paris. "*Quelle mauvaises nouvelles! ils m'ont dit.*" Their alarm at the reported Congress at Chatillon sur Seine, and Lord Castlereagh, &c., has to-day of course a little subsided in consequence. A peace with Bonaparte would ruin them for ever. If Paris now declares itself, on the other hand, it will spread, and the whole business be at an end in their favour, I think. If not, it is clear their party is very small, and their interests forgotten.

The 18th, Friday.—Still Lord Wellington not returned, but we had some news of what has been

done on the right. The French retired skirmish-
ing, but would never stand to let us charge. They
were obliged to remain longer than they wished to
cover some guns which they carried off; and also,
the evening before last, they intended to take up
their ground for the night in a position which
Lord Wellington thought it would suit him to
drive them from; by doing this late in the day
they were obliged to resist more than they probably otherwise would, if they had expected it,
and been prepared for the retreat. We have taken
about ten or twelve officers prisoners, and about
two hundred men. Some say we might have had
as many thousands, could we have been two hours
sooner. These things are always, however, said.
Supposing that we had been two hours' sooner, the
French would have been just where they were;
and it is forgotten that if we had moved sooner,
they might probably just have done the same
thing. We have ourselves sustained some loss, and
that in a greater proportion of officers than men. I
am told, about a hundred and twenty men. General
Pringle is shot in the breast,—an awkward place,
but they hope not badly, considering the situation.
General Byng's aide-de-camp, Captain Clitherow,
is killed, and, I believe, Lieutenant Moore, of
the artillery. Aides-de-camp and Brigade-Majors

have suffered much of late ; Lord Wellington's are uncommonly fortunate. I have heard also that Lieutenant-colonel Bruce is wounded, a Bevan (Major or Colonel in the Portuguese service), and some subalterns of the two brigades of General Byng and General Pringle, the only two engaged.

By the last accounts, Lord Wellington's head-quarters were at Garris, near St. Palais, and the French are driven across the Bidouge, a river that runs into the Adour below the Gaves, and near Grammont's place, Guiche, of which he is duke. The French have only pickets on our side the first Gave, the Gave d'Oleron, when they are driven across. I think Lord Wellington will return here to-morrow to see about the grand bridge and the operations on this side, which are the most ticklish. Elphinstone would have his bridge ready to-morrow night if the materials get round in time from Passages, and provided one vessel is got out from our river here, for one could not be moved over the bar yesterday, from its having the guns on board, which are to be dropped into the Adour, to assist in moving the vessels of the bridge. By taking out the guns this difficulty may be got over, but the wind is not fair from Passages. This is the worst part of the business, for though the elements alone may be to blame, still Lord Wel-

lington, if his plans are thwarted, will be in a rage
with ——. He banishes the terms difficulty, impossibility, and responsibility, from his vocabulary.

The moment he has done on the right, he wants
to be ready here, as he knows that as long as he
remains there, the attention of the French is drawn
that way, and the same when he shall return here.
We have now no troops here. The Guards have
moved into Bidart, and we have now permanently
occupied Biaritz in front of Bayonne; General
Vandeleur sleeps there, and all his horses un-
saddled. The light division have crossed the
Nivé. The fifth moved a little more to their
right, to occupy part of the ground of the light
near Arbonne and Arauntz, towards Ustaritz; and
the third division, under General Picton, have gone
up to St. Jean Pied de Port, but without oppo-
sition hitherto. The Adjutant general, when he
went himself over to the hospital stations of Fontarabia and Passages, routed out about fourteen
hundred convalescents, and malingerers, &c., and
they passed through here for their regiments yesterday, for every man is wanted now. Unluckily,
no reinforcements have arrived from England;
why, we cannot say, for the wind is fair, and the
papers say they sailed a month since, and the
regiments have had notice of their intended

arrival. The artillery also expect five hundred
horses, which would now be an inestimable treasure, as many are going and getting weak. There
are also about six thousand Portuguese ready to
join in Portugal, but who remain for want of
transport, as I am told ; this is unlucky, as they
were well-seasoned recruits.

It is curious that even latterly, ever since we
left our mountains, almost all our advanced troops—
the advanced line—has been Portuguese ; they not
only stop our deserters, but go off very much less
themselves. From the terrible loss of oxen, we
are all now, officers and all, in this neighbourhood,
living upon salt rations, sea-beef and pork. Luckily
for me, however, we can now buy a little fresh
meat. I find, though I like it, that this salt meat
does not agree with me. We cannot carry it to
the other division, so those who are near the sea
must eat it. I am terribly vexed with myself for
not having desired you to send me out a good
map of France, as I have only the department on
this side the Adour, and the whole seat of the
war is now France. I should like to have got
the abridged or reduced Casini, which is used here
and liked, a map about five or six feet by four or
five, and Stockdale's vicinity of Bayonne, taken
from Casini's large one. These two would have

been a treasure, now we are likely to move ; and I conclude Stockdale will go on publishing some more of Casini to follow us up.

We have begun to establish a recruiting party at head quarters, to select out of the French deserters good subjects for the *Chasseurs Britanniques*, &c. I hope it will answer, but I must say I have my doubts. In the meantime, I shall have to play the part of a magistrate, and swear them all in. Our news from Bayonne to-day is, that a courier arrived yesterday express from Paris in sixty hours ; of course he brought something very important. The story in Bayonne is, that the negociation and congress is broken up already, and this is now considered most excellent news here, excepting by a few soldiers of fortune, and real lovers of their trade, who think it would flourish much better after a peace with Bonaparte than with the Bourbons. What a contrast between the *Moniteur* a year and a half since about Moscow, &c., and the late ones about the works round Paris, and the room left—eighteen inches—for the *piétons* only to pass, &c., and the immense zeal and activity : *Deja on voit les embrassures pour quatres canons.* You will have seen all this, however, and have been as much amused, no doubt, as we have been.

I have just seen Major D——, who is returned from the right.   He says we have been well received in general, and found a tolerable supply of everything in the new country we have been in. If the inhabitants will but stay, they will find a good market for everything, instead of losing the produce for nothing ; and stragglers, single plunderers, &c., dare not commit depredations on the houses in that case.   The people here are in despair at the expected entrance of the Spaniards. We have now shops in abundance, and a good market, and can, with plenty of money, procure most things ; and now we are on the point of being off.

18*th February, later.*—I have just been with Elphinstone, and seen all his drawings and plans for the grand bridge.   They seem very good, and the whole will be ready by Sunday morning, provided the naval gentleman can carry his vessels in ; but he thinks that will not do on account of the tides before Wednesday.   Six or seven small boats are to be carried from here on carriages ; these are to be launched, and are to tow across the first party on rafts, which are made by some platforms placed on the pontoons.   This first party I would rather not accompany.   To show you how little Lord Wellington listens to objections, and how he rather likes to cut up the routine work, I may mention that Elphinstone told him the quantity of plank necessary would take time, and make a delay. "No," says he, "there are all your platforms of your batteries which have been sent out, in case of a siege. Cut them all up." "Then when we proceed with the siege, what is to be done!" quoth Elphinstone. "Oh, work your guns in the sand until you can make new ones out of the pine-wood near Bayonne." So all the English battering platforms have been cut up accordingly.

At Elphinstone's I met the Admiral, who came round to-day to assist, and some small vessels have arrived with him. We have now Sacoa choked full, and quite a flotilla in the open bay, with a wind right on shore into the bay. I only hope it will not take to blowing hard in this direction whilst our operations are going on. The battering train and siege apparatus are also arrived at Passages from St. Andar; this has been done quite snug, even Elphinstone did not know of their coming until here they were.

Letters are come in from the right : all has gone on well there. The French are driven quite across the Gave de Mauleon or Soiron, as it is called in my map, a little river which is the left branch of the Gave d'Oleron, and runs into the Gave d'Oleron below Oleron town. The Adjutant-general writes, that the French have given up all that at present was wanted in that direction. Adieu !

Saturday, the 19*th.*—To-day we have a French bulletin sent in to us of a victory over the forces of the Allies, the Russian army destroyed, and the French in pursuit—baggage, cannon, all taken. This is awkward when we expected daily to hear of the Allies in Paris, and it will have a bad effect on the cause in France, even if it is only a slight check to the allied armies. Our French here have their proclamations printed, and *fleurs-de-lis* are being made. Lord Wellington says they must wait until he is more advanced before they begin to circulate them. He is expected back to-day. The weather has been very cold again, and sleet or snow has just begun to fall. I have also to-day to acknowledge a letter from you of the 8th, and papers from the 2nd to the 8th inclusive.

I have to report myself continuing nearly well. I have walked myself into tolerable condition again, and hope to take the field without risk or suffering. I am just interrupted by a noise at the Provost guard opposite and the arrival of about a hundred and eighty French prisoners escorted by a party of the 57th regiment, who might

with great advantage change clothes with the
French. The latter are in general very well
clothed, and very fine young men, a few older
soldiers amongst them in particular. The young
conscripts look rather pale and sickly. Our
57th men are absolutely in rags and tatters,
here and there five or six inches of bare thigh or
arm are visible through the patches ; some have had
only linen pantaloons all winter through. They
all get their new clothing to-morrow at Sacoa ; the
whole regiment comes down here for that purpose,
and then nearly the whole will have had their
clothing this year, all but one or two regiments.

Later, 4 o'clock.—Lord Wellington is just returned from the right, and so eager is he when
anything is in hand, that I saw him going round
by the Admiral's and Colonel Elphinstone's before
he went home on horseback, after a tolerably long
ride too. The Admiral he carried off with him.

20th February, post-day.—The first thing I saw
this morning in my walk on the wall was Lord
Wellington looking at the sea at half-past seven.
The wind was strong, right into the bay, and not a
ship could stir. He soon saw the Admiral come
out also to look, and carried him off home. I saw
Lord Wellington about some Courts-martial just
now, and expected to be rather snubbed ; but he

was in high good humour, and I was, of course, as short as possible. The moment is, however, ticklish. Had the gale this morning increased, none of the ships in the bay, I think, could have stood it. It was right into the bay against them, and they were anchored within two hundred, three hundred, or four hundred yards of the shore. The slip of an anchor or breaking of a cable would have been destruction, and we have now a wreck on each side of the bay, which is ominous and terrific to strangers and new-comers.

Later.—Lord Wellington is already beginning to provide against the failure of his bridge plan from winds and tides, and I understand will not wait above a day or two on this account. I hear that arrangements are in consequence forming to make the main movement still by the right altogether, and to come round on Bayonne in case the bridge scheme will not very speedily answer.

END OF VOL. II.

LONDON:
Printed by Schulze and Co., 13, Poland Street.

1418880R0

Printed in Great Britain by
Amazon.co.uk, Ltd.,
Marston Gate.